D0292961

The Boyle Chronicles: Book Three: Bertha

by

Ronald "Ron" Baldwin

Other Titles by Ronald 'Ron' Baldwin

The Boyle Chronicles: Book One: James & Sarah
The Boyle Chronicles: Book Two: James & Judith

Visit Web Site –
www.gbronline.com/ronbaldwin2/books.htm

© Copyright 2005 Ron Baldwin.
All rights reserved. No part of this publication may be reproduced, stored in a retrieval system, or transmitted, in any form or by any means, electronic, mechanical, photocopying, recording, or otherwise, without the written prior permission of the author.

Note for Librarians: A cataloguing record for this book is available from Library and Archives Canada at www.collectionscanada.ca/amicus/index-e.html
ISBN 1-4120-7036-8

Printed in Victoria, BC, Canada. Printed on paper with minimum 30% recycled fibre. Trafford's print shop runs on "green energy" from solar, wind and other environmentally-friendly power sources.

PUBLISHING™

Offices in Canada, USA, Ireland and UK
This book was published *on-demand* in cooperation with Trafford Publishing. On-demand publishing is a unique process and service of making a book available for retail sale to the public taking advantage of on-demand manufacturing and Internet marketing. On-demand publishing includes promotions, retail sales, manufacturing, order fulfilment, accounting and collecting royalties on behalf of the author.

Book sales for North America and international:
Trafford Publishing, 6E–2333 Government St.,
Victoria, BC v8t 4p4 CANADA
phone 250 383 6864 (toll-free 1 888 232 4444)
fax 250 383 6804; email to orders@trafford.com
Book sales in Europe:
Trafford Publishing (uk) Limited, 9 Park End Street, 2nd Floor
Oxford, UK ox1 1hh UNITED KINGDOM
phone 44 (0)1865 722 113 (local rate 0845 230 9601)
facsimile 44 (0)1865 722 868; info.uk@trafford.com
Order online at:
trafford.com/05-1947

10 9 8 7 6 5 4 3 2 1

INTRODUCTION

At nineteen years Bertha is a beautiful, intelligent creation of pioneering parents and an incessant desire to learn and experience. Having set high standards for herself, she finds it a struggle to maintain her life's course as she has dreamed it should proceed. Close reading of her diary kept since the age of nine, shows a determination to attain her goals beset with natural and human tragedy. With a passion for life and a fearlessness not often seen in females of the times, she takes on all.

Born a twin girl, with brother David first born, on 10 October 1780. She came into this world a demanding baby.

Her mother, Sarah Boyle, a pioneer on the frontier in upstate New York, was a beautiful woman with flashing dark eyes that captured Bertha's father, James, the first time they met. He was a handsome man with black hair and winning ways. Together they had moved to the frontier to make their own way in life. Tragedy struck first with an attack on James by a panther, followed by a still birth and then the killing of Bertha's twin brother David, by the panther's mate. A year later, Sarah is killed in a vindictive attack by local Indian haters.

Prior to the death of Sarah, Bertha had been taken to her maternal grandmother's for raising and was not present the night her mother was killed. Grandmother Barton, happy to impart gentile ways in her rough and tumble granddaughter, teaches her the ways of polite society with an eye toward marrying her to a professional man of means, when the time comes.

As a growing child, Bertha absorbed all the book learning placed before her, but she insisted on learning the skills necessary to running a household, as she had seen her mother do, contrary to her grandmother's wishes. Mrs. Barton believed that in a family of means, the hired help did everything required to run a household.

When her father remarries, her new stepmother removes her to their home in Cooperstown, N.Y. and begins teaching the child an independent way of thinking that more nearly suits her personality, while continuing her literary and basic education. A strong bond develops between the two females. Here Bertha broadens her perspective, learning from their association with the Cooper family, which placed a large library at her disposal.

By her teen years she is graceful and well spoken, despite her lack of extensive formal education. She draws the romantic interests of virtually every young male around. Aware that she can do better than the local bumpkins she manages to avoid any serious relationship, keeping her sights on higher goals. Beautiful with a full figure, topped with dark hair above dark piercing eyes she has been informally, judged the 'most beautiful woman' in the settlement; she is independent of thought and spirit.

An accomplished writer, her letters for her father's business showcasing her abilities and mind, a local group of parents have turned to her to teach in the new school, the first in this part of the New York wilderness. The school has shut down for Christmas and New Year when tragedy again, strikes her family.

A New Years eve fire has sweep the Boyle property and killed James, her father and Judith, her much loved stepmother. Bertha is left to oversee the remaining Boyle family.

Chapter One
Arrangements

Standing at the graves of her father and stepmother, Bertha doesn't try to hold back the tears. Their deaths have come without warning, leaving her, temporarily, homeless with two brothers and a sister to see to, a heavy burden for a young woman of nineteen years.

After the fire had swept through the family home, killing James and Judith, she has had to decide whether to let the authorities in Cooperstown spread her siblings among those willing to take them or do whatever necessary to keep them together. She has opted for the later.

Writing of the tragedy to her uncles in Worcester, she had received a missive encouraging her to bring them all to their farms. She wrote back of her intent to remain where she is, fulfill her obligations to the school and see to the proper raising of her siblings.

James' brothers then make plans to come to her aid and attend their brother's burial. They had written of their intentions and Bertha has delayed the services until they arrived. It is early March as they are all gathered for the graveside service.

Standing with her back to the brisk wind her siblings gathered around, head held high, as the tears flood down her cheeks and drip to her bodice, she presents a picture of determination. Inside, her heart aches beyond possible immediate repair. The children are all sobbing, as the minister from Cooperstown, come down for the purpose, reads from the Bible and offers a prayer for the souls of the dead and the survivors.

The crowd begins to work its way down the hill to the waiting buggies and wagons. Richard Jewell has stayed in the background, available for support both emotional and physical. While she has often acknowledged his presence, she has remained aloft. He steps beside her now, offering a hand, she takes it with a warm squeeze and look that makes his heart leap.

Her uncles have asked that they meet in Richard's office, near the inn. Richard guides her and the children to a buggy he intends will take them to the meeting.

There her Uncle Charles indicates that they all need to pay attention, and then he begins, "Every one of you children is welcome at mine or your Uncle Michael's home. In fact, it is our heartfelt hope that you will chose to leave with us on the morrow."

Turning to Bertha, he continues, "Should any of you desire to stay with your older sister, we will understand. Being a strong, young woman of some means and good background, we know that she can take good care of you."

Richard wonders what 'of some means' means. He is aware that she will probably inherit some cash, but it is traditional that the first born son receives his father's lands, business, etc.

Going on, Charles, adds, "Whatever support or help she might need, Michael and I are prepared to offer." Standing nearby, Michael nods his head in acquiescence.

"Little Charles is too young to make such a decision," Michael joins in, "In his case we will let Bertha keep him with the option to join us later, if he so wishes. Nancy, while being accepted as a full member of the Boyle family, can choose to come with us, stay with Bertha or ask to be joined with her blood relatives where ever they may be."

David James, nearly silent since relating what he had seen at the fire days ago, looks up at his uncle Charles and says, "I want to go with you," in an unemotional voice that tells of his anguish and troubled mind.

Bertha steps to him and wrapping him in her arms, says, "It's alright, we will visit in time and you can come here."

"Bertha, we are aware that you have your own means and are prepared to assist you in anyway we can as always."

"If you will just keep doing as you have and assist in the sale of my lands," she states, "I will be having a house built for us near my school, where I can raise my brother and sister. Since David James will be inheriting father's lands and business, what do you recommend be done with them?"

Looking at Richard, Charles asks, "Do you want to continue on here in David James' behalf?"

"Wouldn't have it any other way," he says, "I owe his father much and will help in any way possible."

"Well, that should tie up the loose ends, except for Nancy." Turning to her he asks, "Do you understand what we have said?"

Lifting her head to look into his eyes, she states loudly, "I want to stay with Bert!" Then embarrassed that she has spoken so loudly, lowers her head and whispers, "If it's alright."

Sweeping the little red-head up in her arms Bertha bursts out, "Sure it's alright, honey, I want you to stay." Then she says, "Uncle Charles, I can't thank you and Uncle Michael enough for all you've done for me. That you have come all the way here to be with us means so much." She then gives each a hug and kiss on their cheeks.

Turning to Richard, reaching for his hand, she continues, "You are an invaluable friend to this family and I probably can never repay you for standing by." Tears slip down her cheeks as she helps the small ones into their coats. "We must say goodbye to Uncle Charles, Uncle Michael and David as they will be leaving in the morning, early."

Hugging David to her again, she admonishes him to mind Uncle Charles and to write often. She promises to write back. Reaching out for Richard's hand she turns for the door.

Each of the little ones says goodbye to David and get hugs from their uncles, and then leave for the various families that are caring for them until the new house can be built.

Bertha gives Richard a hug and promises to meet him here tomorrow, early. She wants to see her brother and uncles off in the morning.

Bertha, deciding to be frank with Richard, asks him to take her to Brink's for dinner that very evening after her uncles have departed. The boldness of her request aside, he is more than willing to share a meal with her. Picking her up at the Young's, they enter the dining room and find it occupied by several guests of the inn, the only empty table away from earshot of others is the one at which her father was shot. Without mention of the incident or hesitation she allows him to seat her and order their food. The blood stains have been mostly removed from the rough plank floor.

They make small talk through most of the meal then she opens up, "You should know a few things about me." She has his rapt attention.

"My mother was killed by racist Indian haters while I was at my grandmother's in Worcester, Massachusetts. My father was shot at this very table by the brother of one of my mother's assassins and I killed him right here.

I was only nine when I was taken east. My formal education was in a school there. My mother taught me my letters and numbers. I have moved my education forward by reading extensively. My letters I have practiced by keeping a journal that thankfully, was with me the night of the fire. My stepmother, Judith, worked with me to broaden my perceptions and perspectives. At his death, my father's father left me his farm and two stores and a considerable amount of money. In agreement with my father and Judith all that they had is to go to their son, David James, who has already inherited his maternal grandfather's farm back in Massachusetts. Both of us are independently wealthy. Our uncles see to our lands and the stores.

I tell you all of this so that you know how I can have a house built and purchase things for the school. You, I know, are aware of my independent attitudes. I take nothing for granted, yet I expect the best of every one. I am in a position where I can see to all my material needs and wants."

Listening to her go on Richard begins to wonder where in her life he might fit. Any other woman looking for a mate looks to him to be the provider; this is going to be a different situation, indeed.

He remains quiet as she continues, "I know that you would like a closer relationship now. Because I need to get a home set up for the children and keep the school on schedule I don't anticipate much time to give to you exclusively. Please don't misunderstand me; I would dearly love to give to you all that you desire. I feel to be straight with you, I need to say these things."

"Bertha, I will admit that I love you dearly and desire that we eventually marry. But, I have no intention of pushing you or of making any demands, I just want to be there for you, I can be patient," he replies, smiling at her serious visage.

"I have no idea how long I'll need," she states.

"You have as long as necessary."

Her face softens perceptibly, "I don't want to hurt you, ever. But I can make no promises, now."

Again, smiling, he offers, "When you are ready I'll be here." He reaches for and squeezes her hand.

Matching his smile, she squeezes back, "I certainly hope so," she murmurs.

Returning her to the Youngs', they are seen exchanging passionate kisses before he rides off to his folks. Arriving there he is visibly serene. Knowing that he has been with Bertha, his folks are happy for him. His mother inquires, "How soon will she have a place for her brother?" She has been delighted to have the youngster around, but has to admit that he is a handful, showing the Boyles' propensity to look into everything.

"The crew will start on the house with good weather, shouldn't take more than three months," he allows. Just then Charles comes toddling by and Richard reaches and picks him up, "You have a very special sister and I intend to marry her!" The child only smiles and gurgles his pleasure at being swung about.

Looking at his mother's inquisitive face Richard says, "Not too soon." She goes back to her sewing. Having heard, but remaining silent, his father nods to himself about his son's good senses and goes back to his reading.

Early schools on the frontier were organized by the settlers' awareness that the children needed at least a basic education. The older boys were given further training in preparation for secondary schooling should the parents desire it. With no guidelines from governmental authorities each school tended to gain its worth by the quality of the teacher hired. These primitive schools were of the one room type, usually with poor lighting and little in the way of equipment other than a large fireplace for heat, the wood supplied by various farmers, in rotation. Being organized by cash poor farmers for the most part, there was little money available even for the very basics. The buildings often burned and had to be replaced.

Built in 1798, Bertha's school is atypical, located where it is, to serve children that could walk to it. The lower walls are of logs topped with a frame structure that is covered with an open rafter roof. Windows consist of oiled paper stretched on the frames. The floor where the students set on wooden benches is of boards laid on leveled ground. The floor at the head of the room is of hewn logs laid close, giving the teacher a higher elevation from which to teach. Along the back, the log wall has been drilled allowing pegs that support a long board that acts as a common desk. One door, to the east allows entrance and egress. The rest of that wall is covered by the large stone fireplace. Outside and around in back is a woodshed and outhouse divided in the middle with two doors, one each for boys and girls over a common hole in the ground.

Having lost much of her papers and some books when her parents' home burned, Bertha, sets about recreating or getting replacements for what was lost. On the morning her uncles left she gave Charles a list of her needs and they promise to send them along with whatever books are available.

Meeting with the men that her father and McVean have employed as loggers, mill hands and carpenters she and Richard encourage them to stay on and continue in his employ. A one story home is planned to be built next to where Isaac and Nancy had built, construction to begin as soon as the weather permitted.

While Bertha sets about her tasks, Richard takes a good look at the logging, milling and land sales situations.

Good foremen on the logging sites and at the sawmill assure that all goes well. While a few men still worked as 'bounded labor' most of these workers worked for wages and are content to continue that arrangement. The head miller at the gristmill has run it for years. It comes down to the land sales business that needs immediate attention. Fully understanding the property line and paperwork aspects, he nonetheless, feels out of his element promoting and making sales. Remembering all that James had shown him he is sure that with time he will get the hang of it.

To get his feet wet he rides to Cooperstown to register the latest sales. While there he visits with Judge Cooper's son, Richard, who is handling the land sales they are charged with, when his promoter father is away. The meeting is amicable and they part on the promise to keep each other informed and that he carry the Coopers' condolences again to Bertha.

(Meant, primarily, to instill the basics of reading, writing and arithmetic a rural school is limited or improved by the extent of the education of its headmistress, or headmaster as it may be. Many are organized with both. The headmistress teaches in Summer when the older boys are working. The headmaster teaches in the Winter when the older boys are idled by the weather.)

Bertha has agreed to teach both Summer and Winter, being at the time housed by her father, it was felt and agreed to, that her safety as a female could be attended to under those circumstances. Now with her father gone, some that helped organize the school voice concern at her teaching young men un-chaperoned. A meeting is held in the school on Saturday following the burial.

The concerns come out as to the appropriateness of her position and her safety as a female. Bertha, in attendance, listens politely as her neighbors discuss her situation. She knows that should the concerns be paramount in their thinking, that she will not be allowed to teach in the Winter when boys over twelve would be expected to attend.

Also at the meeting is the new sawyer, who had bought the McConell house, and his young wife, due with child in the Spring. Casting about for an answer Bertha offers, "If there are two adults present each day would that allay the concerns?" A buzz of discussion goes through those assembled; they decide to hear her out.

"I had expected to hire someone days when I am teaching, to see to Nancy and Charles. Putting some credence in your concerns I could bring them and their nanny here with me. Perhaps she could assist me and there would be two adults present." Right off she can see that her idea goes well with those less concerned, but those that had shown the most concern are still skeptical.

"Who would pay this second woman? And who would it be?" someone calls out.

"It would be my responsibility," Bertha counters, "And I had Mrs. Martin in mind," looking at the fairly new comer to the community.

"Me?" she reacts looking at her husband for his guidance. Pausing, then seeing that it would mean that his wife is not home alone and a small income might be derived, he says, "It would be fine with me, Ann."

For herself, new wife and pregnant, Ann likes the idea and nods her acceptance. Being new to the settlement and living away from most of the others she is glad to share the day with Bertha.

Standing up, her husband states, "Miss Boyle, seeing as we live close to the school and your new home will be built next to ours we were thinking that we would offer to board you and the children until your home is completed."

"It would appear that these arrangements would quiet everyone's fears," states the head of the organizing group, if no one has other concerns let's all go home? Miss Boyle, we'll leave you and the Martins to work out the details."

Everyone departs except Bertha, Richard and the Martins. Gathering together Bertha apologizes for not consulting with them earlier. They accept and are just glad that they could help keep the school open it being that they would have need of it in a few years. They have heard nothing but good about Bertha's teaching and have every hope that their children might attend her school.

"When is your baby due," Bertha asks.

"The doctor said in June," her husband answers for her. She looks at Bertha and smiles with a nod.

"Nancy is two as well as Charles, so they won't be much of a fuss and I look forward to your company. I certainly am grateful for your offer and would like to reopen the school on Monday if possible. The young men that I expect were with me last winter and we shouldn't expect any trouble. If it's alright with you, Richard and I will gather up the children and meet you at your home."

"I am so happy that we can do this," Ann gushes.

In a short time, they have arrived at the Martins' with the children where they are shown two rooms, one for the children and the other for Bertha.

Settling the children and herself in is a simple process as they have very little to bring with them, all their clothes, toys and furniture were destroyed in the fire. Half of what they bring has been donated by the community to help them in their need. Soon a shipment arrives from Bertha's stores in Massachusetts. Along with clothing for her and the two children she has had beds sent. Replacing the four poster with goose-down mattress that she had felt like royalty in with another of like construction, Bertha now feels like life is gaining some normalcy. Once the new house is nearly completed she plans to send to her uncles for additional furniture and necessary household goods.

Richard finds himself busy doing surveys and dealing with several potential buyers of undeveloped lands. One area in particular in the Otego Patent involves the resale of lands sold by the Coopers to land speculators, along the east branch of the Otsdawa Creek north of Huntsville. The buyer wants to own an area where he can raise a millpond to furnish water to several mills.

As often as time allows Richard stops by the school or the Martins' to spend time with Bertha. She is grateful for the distraction and often on a weekend has gone horseback riding with him. Avoiding the site of the fire they most often ride across the bridge at the McVeans' and on up through the settlement to his parents place up the Oneonta Creek.

While pleased to see these two fine young people drawn together, his parents observe a reserve in Bertha toward marriage that bothers them. They have acknowledged it to each other but have resolved to remain silent, as far as Richard is concerned, and see what comes of things.

Ann has become a great help to Bertha at school and a welcome overseer of Nancy and Charles. The two children are quite happy, finding the whole situation to be a big adventure. Playing together before the fireplace in the school they have begun to look to each other as brother and sister, not having any memory of their separate mothers. They look at Bertha as filling that role and Ann as an aunt.

Winter's cold gives in to Spring rains and for days the river rises until it threatens the mills again. Unable to operate the mills with such volumes of water rushing down stream, Richard sends both crews home. Idled by the bad weather several of the men begin hanging out at Brink's, including the sawyer, Martin.

A few years older than Ann, Henry Martin has in the past felt he had good reason for drinking. Back on the Schoharie where they had come from, he had lost his first wife and child to smallpox soon after the child's birth. For most of the following year he was lost to drink. Finally pulling himself together he had convinced the pretty fifteen-year-old daughter of a neighbor that he had straightened up and talked her into marriage. Their months together prior to moving here, were good months and Ann has come to believe that she has married a good man. So that first evening when he doesn't come home from work at the usual time, shocks her. When he does show up later, obviously drunk, she makes the mistake of yelling at him in that condition. Bertha, alerted by the outburst, listens to the exchange of words ringing through the house, and then steps from her room into the kitchen where the two antagonists are in heated debate. Her presence dampens the rhetoric and Henry flies out the door into the yard.

Ann glaring at his departing back, yells, "I will not put up with a drunk! I saw my father beat my mother when he got like this and you can just stay out there until you sober up!" Turning to Bertha she attempts to apologize for the outbursts and Bertha waves her off.

"I have never heard two married people yell at each other like that, it is I should apologize for interfering."

"My paw often beat my maw when he'd been drinking, which he did quite regularly, and when she would run away, he'd beat me and my brother," Ann explains, "Henry promised me he would never drink again before I'd marry him. I intend to hold him to his word!"

"Did he strike you?"

"No, but I saw that same look paw would get. I won't have him start! I'll kill him first."

"Come sleep with me tonight. I'm sure that in the morning everything will be alright."

Next morning a disheveled Henry, cold from sleeping in a horse stall out back, taps at the kitchen door as the two women prepare the children for the day, "Can I come in for breakfast?"

"Yes, if you cook it yourself, Henry Martin!" states his wife, "I have no time for a drunk."

Stepping inside he looks to Bertha and sheepishly apologizes for his actions. She looks him in the eye and just nods, wanting him to understand that she in no way condones his mistakes. The two women, hurrying the children before them, brush past him and out the door into a driving rain.

The river below surges on, full in its banks and threatening to breach them soon. At the homes and inn a short way from the river, concern has spread as the settlers awoke to this hard rain. Brink gathers up the early customers and some neighbors and sets about building a dike to protect his buildings, he has seen the river rage past his doorstep before. Those beyond and below, mostly workers with log cabins, will have to fend as best they can. Some are already moving their children and animals to higher ground to the north. Other Spring floods have occasioned a stream of water through these flats but only deep enough to harm the lowest places. Usually caused by ice jams they had quickly receded with the jams going out. Never has anyone seen the river this high from just rain, and more coming.

The bridge the McVeans had built below the mills is impassable by mid-morning as the water rises as high as its deck. This effectively cuts the settlements South of the river off from those of the main hamlet. Richard, helping to build the dike, knows that he can't get to Panther Mountain or them to him.

At school, Bertha keeping one eye on the weather, dismisses the students at mid-day. She is concerned about them having to cross the creek between the school and where the cluster of homes is. No bridge has yet been built and when it rains the log that spans the creek seems a bit treacherous with the rushing stream below lapping at the underside. Most times a fall off the log meant a splash in a shallow pool under it but when the water off the mountain comes rushing down in a rain storm, a fall means a certain disaster as the victim is carried down to the river.

Today the adults keep the smaller children together and they approach the crossing with particular concern as the water roars down the mountain. Normally four or five steps gets one across the top of the log, but with the distraction of the rushing waters a person can quickly get disoriented and misstep. Bertha and Ann decide that they should carry each child they can across. The older heavier ones should cross between the adults holding their hand, fore and aft.

The headmistress makes the first crossing and back without incident. Ann does the same. A second and third trip gets the smaller ones across where they huddle together against the rain.

Taking one of the older girls first, they form a human chain and complete the crossing with only a small slip of one foot by Ann. Leaving the girl to watch over the little ones, Bertha and Ann, holding hands to steady each other return for the last girl. As they are forming the human chain, one of the boys, wet and bored at watching this process and having crossed many a stream by himself, bolts past the females and hops on the log. Upon his third stride he losses his footing on the wet wood. Seeming to hang momentarily above the on rushing waters he falls into the maelstrom of tumbling water, sticks, limbs and stones. Standing closest to him, Ann steps forward and grasps for a flailing arm. Grabbing hold as he is swept under the log she is pulled down belly first and remains on the log only due to the hold the girl between her and Bertha has.

Shouting for the nearby boys to grab them, Bertha struggles to pull them back. The errant boy is entirely out of sight; except for his hand that Ann maintains hold of. The little group struggles like this until an older boy can get to Ann and lying alongside her grasps the boy's arm, together they pull until his head and shoulders rise above the boiling waters. At this point the whole group of them is able to pull him closer to the near side where the water has less force and after a few minutes struggle drag him from the stream.

Exhausted, Ann and the boy who helped her collapse in a heap while Bertha and the others seeing that the boy is not breathing, roll him on his stomach and push on his back, water gushes from his mouth, but still no breath. Bertha not willing to lose a student in this fashion raises him up and slaps him full in the face, hard. He is turned by the blow and coughs, throwing up more water. Gasping for breath he is held closely to her as she looks skyward, "Thank you," she whispers.

The crossing is completed without further incident. The entire rain soaked group is then taken to the Martin home and allowed to warm up and dry some before the children head on home. Henry is there to help and builds a good fire for the purpose.

The two adult females set drinking tea and discussing their good luck. Bertha, concerned for Ann's pregnancy, asks, "Do you feel alright?"

Nodding, Ann, says, "I feel fine."

"Perhaps you should see the doctor, anyway."

Bertha

"She says she's fine and we have no money for a doctor," interjects her husband.

Turning to him, a look of fierceness snapping from her eyes, Bertha states, "You did not see how she strained to save that boy! She will see the doctor and money will not be a concern!"

Cowering from her attack he takes his tea and retires to the front porch, in silence. Bertha takes a deep breath and makes Ann promise to see the doctor as soon as the roads would allow it, not aware that as they had sent the children home, the Susquehanna has breached its banks near the McVean mills and a strong stream is flowing past Brink's inn and down through the fields and forests. Several families have evacuated to higher ground as the rain continues to pour down. The valley is paying a price for all the clearing of the forest that has been done in the watershed.

While those on the mountainside cannot see the breach at the McVean mills, those watching soon see a stream cutting through the low ground crossing the open fields below their high perches. With too much water for its ancient waterway and missing the restricting forest, the Susquehanna is cutting new paths for itself through the deep valley soils. Where the river has been located below the bluffs on the north side of the valley, when this flood subsides it will have a new channel at the base of Panther Mountain on the south side. Else where up and down the valley similar changes to the old riverbed are being wrought. This process included widening of the old riverbed to accommodate the volume of water. Much of the valley is forever changed.

Just below where James Boyle had developed his farm the river has cut off another large loop in its ancient bed and placed nearly 100 acres of the valley floor that was south of the river, north of its new path and left its old course as an 'oxbow' in the land.

The old course at the McVean mills now carries little of the river's full burden; instead it now carries the waters of the Oneonta Creek and several lesser streams. Similar

18

changes in the Susquehanna's riverbed, here and there cut settlers off from large portions of their lands.

Bertha

Chapter Two
Return to the Mountain

Raining for days, the weather suddenly takes a turn for the better. The clouds drift away, a brisk southwest wind brings drying and warmer temperatures. The grasses grow and the trees bud as Spring finally pushes Winter away.

With a drying of the ground, plowing of the fields is just days away. Bertha knows it is time to close the school until planting season is over, so she announces to the students that this will be the last week until the summer session.

In a few days the river subsides and can be forded on horseback. Richard, hungry for her presence, crosses the new channel and rides to the school. Tying up in front he steps to the door. Blocking the light causes all within to look to the door. To those inside he is a tall, dark hulk in the doorway, except to Bertha, who recognizes his shape at once. Disregarding decorum for the time being, she fairly leaps into his arms, much to the delight of the students and Ann who, in a moment of fear, had stepped toward the pistol they have agreed to keep handy.

With no danger present, Ann steps to the front of the room and calls the children's attentions to her, giving the embracing couple a moment to step outside. Practically carrying her, Richard holds her to him as their lips meet. A surge of passion flows over them both as they cling together.

Stepping back a little, Richard can see that her cheeks have a high color to them and her breasts heave with her breathing. He again draws her to him and lowers his lips to hers. He can now feel the fullness of her breasts heaving against his chest.

As she begins to gain her composure she pushes him back, "Mr. Jewell! I am a school teacher!"

"And a mighty pretty one!" As a bevy of giggles issues from the schoolroom, letting them know they are being overheard.

"Whatever brings you up here just now," she asks, straining to gain control of herself.

"Thought it best to check on you once the river became fordable," he smiles.

"Glad you did, but I must get back to my students."

"After classes?"

"We'll be done by four."

"I'll be here."

She returns to the classroom to an array of smiles and giggles. Soon the situation returns to normal, but she can't stop thinking about their embrace. Something had happened that had never happened before. Her mind grapples for an answer that is better looked for in her heart.

The children's attentions are drawn away as a garter snake has slithered up onto the floor near Miss Ann. Seeing their new interest slide across the floor toward her she bends and grabbing it by its tail, heaves it out the door. "Back to your numbers children!" she commands as Bertha resumes her place at the head of the room.

Riding on down river, Richard goes to check on the logging operations. The men who live on this side of the river are working, trying to avoid any mud if possible. Muddy logs are hard on the mill's blade. The river too fast to allow poling of log rafts up to the mill and the road needing several more days of drying before the ox teams can draw wagons through, the men are piling the production.

Aware that their hearts have spoken, Richard rides with mixed thoughts. Should he continue to show patience or should he attempt to move things forward by proposing marriage. His whole being says that he can't control his needs and desires much longer. Pushing the thoughts back he tells himself that they might find an answer this afternoon.

Unable to concentrate, Bertha turns the students over to Ann and steps outside to clear her head. Overhead a red-tailed hawk screeches as it circles looking for a meal then drifts off toward where the Boyle home had stood. Looking up she suddenly thinks, "My mind circles just as you do!" Never afraid of life she always looks for ways to control what is happening to her. For once she is aware that she doesn't have all the answers. She returns to her duties.

Bertha

Come four o'clock Richard returns having consulted with the workers on the hamlet side of the river and concluded that they would have to use boats to ferry men and equipment until plans can be made for a new bridge. Several ideas were passed around and the need to build a substantial structure well above the high water and ice was agreed on but it would take time to be realized. The students had all left and Ann has taken her two charges home when he arrives. Bertha is just closing the building and they walk together toward the Martin home. The stream, now no more than a trickle, can be crosses on a few well placed stones as the log had washed away.

They make small talk as she relates what had happened during the heavy rains. Aware that it could have been she that fell in, Richard makes a note to have the logging crew build a safer way of crossing.

At the house Ann has tea warmed and they all set about the kitchen table. Richard tells Henry that a boat will be coming over at six o'clock in the morning to fetch him and other workers.

Knowing that they wanted to talk, Ann asks Henry to join her in their room and leaves Bertha and Richard alone. Neither quite knows where to start so they set quietly, thinking.

Reaching out to take his hand she says, "We have much to talk about."

"Now?" he looks at her inquiringly.

"Can we wait until Saturday? I am closing the school on Friday and will be where I can think about the future."

"Guess I can wait a couple of days. The boat in the morning will be bringing the men to start on your house. I'll be with them to set the corners." He had arrived, prepared to ask her to marry him should the conversation turn that way. Now he pulls back, willing to wait at least two more days.

Stating a need to get things together for the morrow, he stands to go. She arises with him, still holding his hand. They embrace but the heat of the morning is not allowed to rise. He leaves saying that he will bring an extra horse about

22

seven on Saturday. She steps forward and kisses him a quick goodbye and releases his hand, "I'll be ready," she smiles, "I'd love to go riding."

Saturday morning arrives with a bright warm sun shining down the valley. Here and there a wispy cloud slides across the sky from the west. The red-tailed hawks are active over Panther Mountain when Richard ties up the mounts. Just as he starts for the door Bertha exits with saddlebags in hand, "I packed us a snack," she smiles, obviously enthused about his arrival. A quick embrace and they swing into the saddles. He turns his mount to descend the mountain when she calls out, "This way," and turns up the road.

Surprised, he quickly draws along side of her. Up to now she has not mentioned the fire or shown any interest in returning to the scene of the tragedy. Looking at her with a questioning look, he waits for an explanation.

The horses moving at a leisurely walk, she turns to him, "I feel that I can now face what happened, we'll soon find out."

A few minutes later they top the rise to where the house had stood to be greeted by a small pile of charred timbers, both where the house and barn had stood. The smaller buildings had been entirely consumed, so intense was the fire. The burned over yard and forest behind now showing green splotches as nature reclaims its own. Here and there trees show a little damage but the fire went through so fast it did little harm to the forest as it raced up the mountain. An age old natural method of renewal, fire of this type, does more to improve the overall environment than harm it.

Strolling about the clearing, Bertha remembers what Judith had told her about why she had chosen this place for their home. Looking out over the valley and community below, here and there a wisp of smoke marks the locations of homes in the forest; she begins to think that it would memorialize her father and Judith to rebuild the family home.

Bertha

Turning to Richard she asks, "Is it too late to change where I would like to build?"

"If you're serious I could hire a crew to clean up and begin construction next week," Richard testifies.

"I think it best that we start as soon as possible," she states, making up her mind fully as they stroll about the fire site hand in hand. The bench that James had set near the front edge of the clearing, while charred beckons, they walk there and set silently looking over the valley.

Richard pulls her close and places his arm around her shoulders. With a soft voice he says, "I love you. Will you marry me?"

Knowing that he would ask soon, she settles close to him and responds, "And I love you." Hesitating to answer his question as she mulls it over, she smiles softly to herself, "What ever objection could I have?" passes through her mind. None coming to mind she turns to him and says, "Yes".

A big grin breaks out on his face as his heart leaps! He is at once overjoyed and shows it by leaping to his feet drawing her with him. Taking her in his arms he kisses her again and again while murmuring, "Thanks, thanks, thanks!"

Bertha too is overjoyed, returning his kisses with great passion and clinging as close as possible. "We must do it soon!" she breathes.

All he can do or say is nod in agreement as he feels her body's promise pressed to his, "Soon!"

With that they regain their horses. Walking them down the hill affords them a few minutes to contemplate their decision.

"There is no clergyman in town," Richard states.

"Mr. Jewell, I do believe you are in a hurry!" she spouts with a smile.

"Do you wish to have a fancy service and party?" he asks.

"I think not."

"We could ride to the nearest judge and have him perform the ceremony," he offers, opting for quick action instead of further delay.

"Give me a chance to find an appropriate wedding dress and we can ride to Cooperstown tomorrow and have the Judge preside," she temporizes.

"Then I must find adequate dress myself," he says.

"It would suit me if we could at least dress appropriately," she comments.

This decided they ride to the new ford and cross to the hamlet and the Young's store. Here Mrs. Young throws herself into digging out the best dress in stock and insisting that Bertha allow her to fit it, stating that she can have it done before dark. When she had insisted that her husband order it for stock he had laughed and said that they would never sell such a dress here in the wilderness. Digging around in the stock room she finally comes up with a large box and withdraws a soft pink satin dress that makes Bertha catch her breath. "Now for some petticoats," Mrs. Young states.

Gathering up the dress, several petticoats and Bertha, she takes them all to their residence with an admonition to Richard, "You have Mr. Young get you set, we women have work to do!"

Later, accompanying her to the river crossing, Richard says that he will meet her at the river come first light. Bertha rides to the Martins alone, where she breaks the news. Ann is very happy for her and embraces her as best she can being great with child.

"I can see that you shouldn't be alone," Bertha states. I should get someone to be with you while I'm gone."

"No need, my Henry will be here and the wife of one of the mill hands has offered to assist me. They live just up river, on this side."

"As long as you are comfortable with those plans."

"You just attend to your wedding and give me no never mind. Besides, this little tyke," rubbing her distended belly, might just wait a few more days. "Henry and I have room for you both when you return."

Bertha

With a great deal of joy in her heart Bertha retires to her room to pack a few things. Not sure if they would return to the hamlet soon, she wants to be prepared.

First light finds Richard waiting at the ford for her to show. Trying to be patient he sets watching a great blue heron fishing in the shallows. Successful at catching a fish the bird flies up to a dead branch overhanging the river to enjoy its feast. Richard about to kick his horse into motion sees movement on the opposite side and soon Bertha is riding down the further bank and across the shallow ford.

Side by side they ride up the trail toward Suffrage and Cooperstown, beyond. Taking most of the day to reach Cooperstown, they arrive in late afternoon at the Judge's home. When Elizabeth learns who it is and why they have come she insists on making them comfortable with her in her new home called Otsego Hall, instead of at the inn.

Busy as usual, even on a Sunday afternoon, the Judge was sent for as the young couple was getting dressed. Arriving shortly, and ascertaining the reason for the summons, Judge Cooper soon has them assembled in his study where he performs the ceremony, with many of his children in attendance. Then he promptly returns to whatever he had been doing.

Richard and Bertha, on the other hand, are lost in each other, too much in love to consider what those around them are doing. Much taken back with Mrs. Cooper's hospitality, they are reluctant to leave her company and retire to the room she has so generously made available to them, when she shoos them off, "You two have much to do, we will look for you at breakfast."

With that they make their apologies and retire hand in hand to the room appointed to them. Barely able to get the door closed before they are at each other. Soon empty clothing marks the path to the huge bed, where they join in a passionate embrace, which takes them to heights of pleasure beyond either's imagination.

Lying together sweaty and exhausted as only the sated can be, they remain locked together breathing heavily. Each silently, savoring what has just happened, they know a physical love that hopefully will assure their emotional union.

Morning finds them slightly embarrassed by their nakedness and need to use the chamber pot as they sort though the clothing for something appropriate to wear to breakfast. Richard can be seen stealing an occasional look at her slim full breasted body as she moves about the room. She too finds a moment to appreciate his lithe muscular build.

Properly clothed, at the breakfast table they are greeted with sly, knowing giggles from the Cooper children. The rooms of the older ones being next to and across from the one used by our young married couple it is apparent that the walls had not stopped the sounds of pleasure each had contributed to the night.

A long walk after the meal introduces them to Otsego Lake and its early morning charms. Bertha having seen the lake before, finds a new appreciation of its beauty, as a lover. She knows that to return here each anniversary would renew their passions for each other. To that end she insists they resolve Richard, less a romantic, goes along.

Returning to the Cooper residence they decide to return to home on the following day. Spending the remains of the day chatting with Elizabeth and her children still at home. When the Judge gives them the grand tour that evening they gain a better understanding of this community to their north. The next day finds them mounted early so as to reach home before too late in the day. When they arrive there they have to see Richard's parents with the news then decide where they will live until the house is rebuilt on Panther Mountain.

Turning up the road along the Oneonta Creek that afternoon, they soon ride into Richard's parents homestead. Greeting them from the front porch, it is evident to the Jewells that something special has happened. The ear to ear grin on Richard's face, gives him away.

Pleased that the young couple have at last made a commitment to each other, his folks congratulate them and offer his room as a place for them until they have their own.

Bertha

Having anticipated this, they had talked on the ride and decided to take Ann and Henry up on their offer, it putting them closer to Bertha's school and the work on the new home.

Explaining why, Richard turns his parents and packs a few things he'll need until he gets back. A short time later they cross the river ford and ride to the Martins.

"My but you look radiant," Ann comments to Bertha.

"And you look about to burst!" Berths replies.

"Doctor, yesterday said anytime now," Henry adds, "I have been so nervous I stayed at home just in case."

"That's good," Richard allows continuing, "We can see to the children and Ann, you best get on to work. We'll send for you if anything happens."

"Have either of you seen Jane or William?" asks Bertha.

"Saw him early heading for the river, probably at your office right now", Henry testifies.

"Good then Jane is probably in the cabin", says Bertha, "I want to talk to her about helping with Nancy and Charles when I need to be away and you", looking at Ann, "Can not be expected to deal with them just now."

"They are good children and not much of a bother", Ann says.

"You just concentrate on the work at hand, we will take care of everything else", Bertha states, "Richard and I will walk up to their cabin with the children and be back soon."

As the four of them draw closer to the Ward's cabin, they spot little Samuel playing in the yard. The Boyle children run on ahead yelling greetings to the small boy.

When the adults draw near, Samuel in all innocence says, "Ma told me to stay in the yard while she has company." About that time the front door bursts open and Jonah Preston comes flying out shoving his shirt tails in his trousers. He flees on down hill not stopping to say a word, his eyes averted.

On reaching the door, Jane steps to the threshold fussing with her hair and buttoning her bodice. Behind her Bertha can see the disheveled bed in the corner.

"Why Ms. Bertha do' you look jus' peachy?" she says.

"Don't try to turn our attention from what we just saw!" snaps Bertha.

"What ever do you mean?"

"You have a hard working, good husband that you best see to for your needs", Richard allows, "This community holds no tolerance for immoral behavior."

"No need for name call'n', Jonah is just a friend come call'n'," Jane lies.

"This infuriates Bertha who bursts out, "You had better remember whose land this cabin is built on and who built it!"

Avoiding eye contact by looking at the floor Jane replies, "Yes m."

"I came here to ask for your help watching Nancy and Charles while Ann has her baby or I need to leave. I'm willing to pay."

"Glad to Ms. Bertha. They can play wi' Sam."

"It shouldn't be much with the school closed, but occasionally I may need to leave them with you, especially when Ann's baby comes. I would like to know that I can send them here and there won't be anything going on. I expect to be busy as we are going to rebuild the house on the mountain right away and we just married."

"Yes 'm, deligh't for ya!" Jane says while thinking, "Those tha' got tell'n' those tha' ain't, wha' to do. Well I didn' choose William an' I will sleep wi' who' I please." She smiles at Bertha and Richard and they both see the defiance in her face.

Walking back to the Martins, Richard says, "I will have a talk with Jonah Preston this very day." Perhaps it's best we don't say more to anyone just now. I would not want William to learn of this he is too good a man."

"I will have her removed from my brother's property if I see or hear of her doing this again. This is the second time she has disrespected the Boyle name. My father's memory deserves better."

Chapter Three
The Bear Hunt

Riding to the office Richard sets things in motion to get the Boyle home rebuilt. He then heads to the Preston home and asks to speak to Jonah. His mother indicates that he is as at the gristmill getting corn ground. Richard says, "Fine, I will see him there or on the road in between."

He has nearly reached the gristmill when he meets Jonah with a wagon headed home. On seeing Richard reined up and waiting for him, Jonah at first thinks to hurry on by and ignore him. A better urge causes him to rein in his team and inquire innocently, "Wha' can I do for you?"

Taken aback Richard can't believe that he would try to act as if they hadn't seen him earlier at the Ward cabin. "It's best you not try to fool with me, young man."

"Wha'ever I do is my bus'ness."

"Most times I would agree with you but this disrespects the Boyle family that has tried to help you and the Wards and it disrespects the whole community. You are a good looking lad, find your own wife and leave Jane alone."

"And if I don'?"

"It's best you don't even contemplate ever seeing her again. You get my drift?"

"Don' you folks ever stop push'n' others aroun'?"

"In some cases, no." Richard turns his horse toward the mill and leaves Preston to think about things. When he arrives home his mother asks if Richard found him to which he replies, "Yup". Nothing further is said or asked.

Activity up and down the road past the Martins and Wards precludes any clandestine daytime meetings so Jane and Jonah don't get to repeat their activities. Whenever Jane has been to the hamlet she is with her husband so they are denied access to each other for months.

Work on the house progresses rapidly, with Bertha and Richard making daily inspections and suggestions. In hopes of eliminating a wild fire getting to the buildings

Bertha

Richard has the whole level area cleared as well as down over the hill sides.

Early one morning Henry comes knocking on Bertha's door, "Come quickly, its happening!" he shouts.

Bertha quickly dresses and goes to their bedroom where Ann is obviously in labor. Bertha sends Henry for the neighbor woman who has mid-wife experience. She then sets about making Ann as comfortable as possible and trying to calm the young mother-to-be. Richard is sent to take the two children to the Ward cabin and to get the doctor. By the time the mid-wife arrives Bertha has a supply of water warming at the fire in the kitchen, clean cloths nearby and Ann happy that competent help is near. Henry is banished from the room to pace back and forth in the parlor listening anxiously to every noise from the bedroom. Bertha bustles in and out fetching warm water to bath the new born in. Henry looks at her with an inquiring look which she answers with a smile and goes about her chore.

Soon a squalling of a baby is heard through the bedroom door. Henry waits anxiously by and then Bertha sticks her head out and tells him, "You can come in and see your baby girl and wife now." He fairly bursts into the room. There on their bed Ann lies with the baby at her breast, smiling at him.

The mid-wife is clearing away the bloody cloths and other unpleasant evidence that the birth had not been an easy one. "Mr. Martin, your wife has had a difficult birth and will need lots of rest to recover. The doctor should be here soon and can see to your wife's condition."

At that, Richard returns with word that the doctor had been called out on another birth and would arrive as soon as he could. He then heads for the Ward cabin to fetch the Boyle children. The three children are playing in the yard. As he approaches, Jane steps to the door and asks him to come in. Saying that he has only a moment, that Ann has given birth to a girl and he must get back, he steps into the low, dark room. Behind him Jane pushes the door closed and he turns to face her.

"What can I do for you?" he asks.

"Just this," she whispers putting her arms around his neck and pulling herself up to his lips. For a moment he is taken aback but then grabs her arms, pulls her from him and holds her at arms length.

"Are you out of your mind? Control yourself!"

"Aw, Mr. Richard I only wan' to thank 'e for he'p'n' me an' Will."

"Not that way your not! I have a wife and you a husband, whom I would not cuckold in this fashion. Now I must get the children and be on my way."

"Any time Mr. Richard, any time," she flings after his receding back.

Disgusted, he calls to Nancy and Charles to follow him as he heads down the hill. Disgusted at her actions and disgusted that, for a moment, he had enjoyed her lips on his her body pressed against his.

Back at the Martins he finds them in a heated discussion as to which grandmother they would name the new baby. Ann favors her maternal grandmother Katherine and Henry favors his fraternal grandmother, Eunice. Bertha has remained neutral and Richard is asked to give his choice.

"A girl should have a name that reflects her beauty and potential," he offers. "Therefore I would chose Katherine it being a 'royal' name."

"Henry says, "I can see the wisdom in that but I get to name the boy when he comes."

One day the crew is setting the rafters and ridge pole on the new house when they hear a grunting and snorting coming from the trees in back of the house. Soon the source comes rambling out of the bushes while the workers on the ground find a higher place to be. A large male black bear gets nothing but respect. It rabbles around poking in here and there finding some food not eaten by the workers, before it wanders off back up the mountain. While the horses tied at the barn site had not appreciated it's presence they had not drawn its attention either. The more knowledgeable workers said that the bear must have eaten recently and wouldn't have been a problem unless it felt itself cornered.

Nevertheless, several workers began bringing rifles with them each day.

Upon hearing of the bear's visit Richard calls for a bear hunt the Saturday coming. Word goes out through the settlement for all interested to assemble at the school house early and to bring any dogs capable of chasing a bear.

That Saturday morning finds a dozen men and boys with four long-legged hounds ready to give chase, all are armed with flintlock rifles. Richard organizes the group into two hunting parties. One to head around the ridge and come up mountain just beyond the Boyle gravesites, the other to go up the mountain to the east of the road and the two parties are to meet on the level land straight above them. His plan being to keep the bruin from holing up in a cave above the old cabin site and to push it into the open forest up high where it will most likely tree and they can shoot it. He declares that a successful hunt will terminate in a bar-b-que here at the schoolhouse.

The two parties start out with the dogs sniffing for a trail, the dogs with the eastern party pick up on the bruin's scent first just as they cross the open ground to the east of where the house is being built. The second party hears the other dogs but continue to climb toward the rocky cliffs. The going is quite steep and the men begin to straggle out behind the younger, spryer boys. This has the effect of stringing a long line of hunters up through the forest, which is fortuitous as the other party has turned the bear to the west in an apparent attempt to reach a cave.

The bear, quite capable of out running the dogs has taken a path just above the construction site that is nearly level. This brings it over the ridge near where the old Indian trail dropped down behind the old Boyle cabin. Here the bruin catches the smell of the second hunting party and pauses to look about. It smells the dogs and several humans strung out up and down the mountain. It turns south and heads for higher ground.

The first dogs knowing that they are closer begin making a terrible racket which draws the second set of dogs into the chase. Their howls warn the bear which then turns down hill to the west. Running at full tilt, dogs just behind him, other dogs coming down from the left the bear runs straight at an elderly hunter bringing up the rear of the line.

Hearing the dogs coming before he sees any movement the old hunter stands poised and watchful, rifle raised. The black bear coming down slope is not able to run as fast as it can on the level or up hill, so the first two dogs are about to catch up when the old hunter sees it coming down through the trees. The running bear coming straight on does not present a very good target, causing the hunter to hesitate.

At last firing, the old hunter creases the bear's right rear hindquarter having the effect of causing the bear to shy to the left just as the dogs arrive at its heels. This wild charging group of animals runs right over the old hunter who has thrown up his rifle as a defensive act. For a moment the man, dogs and bear all tumble together. The younger, swifter hunters of both parties are unsure whether to shot or what and just stand watching the dogs now circled around the enraged bear, diving in to bite and being tossed back by the bear's enormous paws.

One of the older hunters coming down through the forest and seeing the tumult shouts for the boys to shoot before the bear kills the dogs. Several rifles bark at the same time and suddenly the forest is quiet except for the growls of the dogs still able to grab at the dead bruin.

Turning to check on the old hunter's fate they find him curled up defensively, apparently none the worse for his adventure. He retrieves his rifle and they all gather around the carcass. It is then field dressed and dragged down to the logging road just above the river. A wagon is soon procured and the bear hauled to the schoolhouse. Upon skinning it they found only one bullet hole where its backbone had been severed and the groove the old man's bullet had caused. At least four had shot simultaneously making it impossible to determine who killed it, so it is decided to give the skin to the school for in front of its fireplace.

Bertha

A fire pit is promptly dug and the carcass spitted above a roaring fire. Word having gone out, soon the women of the settlement begin showing up with various dishes of food to share. The weather is nice and the men carry the school benches outside for seats. One wagon arrives with wide boards and saw horses from the sawmill and soon improvised tables are assembled. By late afternoon the tables groan with food and the smell of burning bear grease permeates the air. Come dark, the school's equipment is returned and folks start gathering theirs, heading home, the bear's skeleton is picked clean and strewn about by the gnawing dogs.

That evening as they watch a red sunset fade in the west, Bertha says to Richard, "I would like to visit my uncles and brother while we wait for the house to be built. I should like to travel on to Boston for a visit."

Aware that she has always wanted to travel Richard allows, "I can put things in order in a day or two, would that suit you? I too would like to see Boston and check on the latest types of surveying equipment."

"I will ask Mrs. Young to take the children as Ann needs more rest and I can't trust Jane to do a good job."

"You certainly can't trust her," he quips.

Busy thinking about the trip, Bertha does not catch the message in his comment. She is making a mental list of what kind of books she needs for the winter session. Several parents had expressed a desire to have their sons prepared for secondary schooling and she knows that her library is sorely lacking in the necessary texts.

Arrangements made, in two days they ride horses up the trail toward Albany with plans to catch a stage coach east. They are welcomed at Uncle Charles' and made comfortable. No longer active in running his store, having turned day to day operations over to his oldest son, Charles has been able to spend time with Bertha's brother David James.

Her uncle reports that he seems adjusted to the loss of his parents and has continued his curiosity about the natural world. At eight years old he shows signs of a brilliant mind yet when Bertha observes him she detects a quiet reserve that he hadn't had before.

As the three of them set talking Charles points out that whenever he has time David can be found in a stone quarry on the old Boyle farm examining the stones and hunting for fossils. This reminds Bertha of a conversation she had overheard between her father and stepmother.

"My father once told Judith of a mine on Panther Mountain that Patrick McVean had told him was rumored to be up there. I believe they both went looking once but nothing came of it."

This has the effect of catching David's imagination and he asks, "What kind of mine Bert?"

"Not sure David. I don't think that Patrick was sure either. The mine's existence seems more rumor than fact."

The boy's fertile mind begins to think about the possibilities. He can barely remember the type of rocks and stones where he was raised but he knows that they might give one a hint of what's hidden beneath Panther Mountain."

In Boston they stay at a popular boarding house while Bertha explores the book stores and talks with anyone she can find involved with education. She gains a perspective of what secondary and university schools look for in their candidates and gains an awareness of which books she needs to help her students toward those goals. She sets about having several books sent to her at the hamlet including anything she can find that covers geology and mining. By the time that they return to her Uncle Charles' they have arranged for several wagons of household goods, furniture, books and surveying equipment to follow them back home.

When they return to Worcester, Charles tells her of an offer for the old Barton farm he has received and recommends that she accept it, which she promptly does adding greatly to her bank account.

With the farm disposed of Bertha asks her uncles one evening at supper, "What should I do with the store? I have no interest in it other than for income. I can always turn to either of you for anything we need at father's settlement. The Young's stock a great deal that is needed." With that statement she verbalizes her feelings of control and responsibility for the greater community.

"In anticipation of this day Michael and I have put together a proposal," Charles says. "We are willing to buy the stock at the store for what you paid for it and move same to our two stores if you would give the building to be used to replace the school house that burned this past month. We have no interest in the building for ourselves and seeing as it now sets on land we no longer have control over we think it best that you dispose of it."

Looking at Richard she hesitates to answer.

"I think it sounds like a good idea," Richard offers.

"Would they call the school 'The Barton School'?" she asks.

"I'm sure it could be arranged," Michael pipes in with a smile. "We thought you would be agreeable."

"I would like to do that to memorialize our grandparents, "How is David's farm doing?" she inquires.

"From what we hear, Mr. Brindles does quite well for him," testifies Charles.

"Do you think that David will ever want to run the farm?" she asks.

"It would be hard to say, but if it's to be disposed of now would be the time. It is a going concern but the value would gain David more, invested in a good bank. Perhaps Mr. Brindles could arrange to buy it?" Charles points out.

"As David's guardians would we be wrong in selling it for him?" she further inquires.

"I wouldn't think so as the principal could be substantial when he reaches twenty-one. There probably would be enough to see him to a university education and a substantial sum left," Charles states.

"Don't be forgetting his holdings on the New York frontier," Bertha reminds them. "He owns the better part of Great Lots # 16 and 17 as well as father's office building. The bank here in Worcester holds the trust James set up for him as well. It was mine until I inherited the Barton estate."

Adding, she states, "Father's business does well under Richard's guidance so David is further enriched by that activity. To consolidate these far flung enterprises I propose that Mr. Brindles be approached to purchase David's farm, failing that, the farm should be immediately placed on the market. I intend to consult with Richard and with his consent I will pay David a fair price for the land business which I intend that Richard will run for both our benefit while I continue to teach."

"Removing your store from our market area will help us to strengthen our stores for our children," allows Michael, "While solving the local school house problem. I think you have a good plan that should help David, yourselves and both communities."

"That you are rebuilding James' home makes us both proud that you are our niece!" comments Charles. "We hope the very best for you and Richard while still continuing to keep the invitations open for all or any of you to move here."

"I can't thank you enough," she states, "For all you've done and I hope that both of you will come to visit. We have much good to show you." With that they all head off to a night's rest.

In their room Bertha says to Richard, "I'm sorry we haven't talked all this out earlier. The conversation just seemed to draw it all out.

"I accepted that our relationship would be different than most from the beginning," he points out, "I do not feel intimidated or left out, as long as we are partners in everything." He leans to her and kisses her. "I love you."

"And I you."

Next morning finds them packing to leave the following day, when David comes to them and asks if he can accompany them. Bertha tells him he will have to wait awhile until the house is built, that right now there is no place for him. The boy is heartbroken until she tells him that they will send for him as soon as the house is ready.

On the ride home Richard says that they will

have to add more rooms to the house plans and Bertha smiling offers that she thought that a very good idea. That come next May they could be rather crowded if they didn't.

Riding along swaying with the coaches pitches and bumps it takes a few minutes for what she has said to sink in. Richard suddenly turns from the view out the window to look into her eyes. Meeting his look, she nods knowingly not wanting to share this moment with the other passengers. He grins broadly, looking out at the passing countryside. Again looking at her he asks, "Are you sure?" She again nods and smiles.

The ride from Albany to the settlement is one of joy as the parents-to-be discuss the coming possibilities and needs that must be addressed. Changes to the house design are discussed and agreed to, thoughts about how long she should work results in Richard allowing that she will know when to quit, that in the meantime she can prepare Ann to take over if necessary.

Actual changes to the house only involved adding more to the second floor and by removing rafters already in place that could be accomplished without much time added to the total construction time. The building should be enclosed by the time the wagons arrive with the furniture.

With the new surveying equipment, Richard hopes to hire a new helper and put William Ward in charge of that portion of his business. On the last day in the Worcester area he and Bertha had visited the bank and transferred the funds into David's account to pay for the land sales and promotion business. On the ride back Bertha has told Richard about an older student that shows great potential in arithmetic, he rides up river to where the family lives to discuss the job with the boy's father.

The Houghtaling family had moved to land south of the river near the mouth of the Charlotte Creek. They had bought the southeastern most Great Lots of the Wallace land patent. When Richard lays out his plan and salary offing, Mr. Houghtaling can see that it will be a fine opportunity for his middle son. The two men agree that the boy should finish this last year of schooling with Bertha, and then start with Richard and William in the Spring.

Next Richard rides to the office and when William comes in from his work, lays out his plan for him to ponder on. The offer includes a nice increase in his salary that could help stabilize his relationship with Jane.

Upon hearing of the job change, Jane pushes for him to accept the offer. That night she brings some of her old passion to their bed and William goes to work next morning with a spring in his step that had been lost with all the arguments night after night. Upon seeing Richard, he accepts the offer.

By late Fall the house is finished and they have moved in with all the children. Charles has a room that he will share with David, Nancy has her own and a room stands empty but for a crib for the coming baby, next to the master bedroom. All these plus a spare room for guests is on the second floor. The main floor has a parlor with a large fireplace, a large dining area with a long, many leaved table, amble kitchen facilities on the east end and a comfortably large office/den for Richard as well as Bertha's library. This room as well as all the rooms on the north side have large windows allowing good views of the valley and hills beyond. The outhouse sets in the same place, out the west or kitchen doors, back against the trees behind the house. Well away are both the wood shed and animal barn. The forest and bushes have been removed well back from all the buildings except the outhouse.

With the valley putting on its fall splendor, the Boyle/Jewell family is completely settled in and awaiting the coming of the New Year and the new birth. Each morning the three children walk down to the Martins where Ann and Katherine join them for the short walk to school across the newly built bridge that spans the now tame creek.

With the crops in, the school is full of small as well as nearly full grown children. Bertha and Ann find themselves exhausted at day's end. Both women push at their husbands to share the household work. Richard is quite amenable but Henry finds it hard to accept that he should help with meals and the little ones after a full day's work. Slowly Ann gets him to help by taking Katherine while she prepares the evening meal. Soon Henry begins to look forward to his time with the baby.

A letter is dispatched to Bertha's uncle Charles that the house is complete and could he recommend the best way to get her brother David to the settlement. About the time a reply was expected one of Charles' sons with his wife and three children arrive with David. The visitors are put up as best they can while Richard and Bertha's cousin cast about for a farm for him to buy. They end up settling on a farm up the Otego Creek in the Hartwick Patent that he buys from Richard Cooper. By cold weather the new Boyle family is settled into a log cabin on a partially cleared farm.

David is moved in with his brother Charles Michael and he begins wandering about the area familiarizing himself with old landmarks. He intends to start an in depth search for the rumored mine on the mountain.

Just when everything seemed to be going well for the settlement the only doctor is killed on his way to a birthing woman up along the Charlotte Creek. Apparently, as no one was around to attest to what actually happened, his horse bolted perhaps frightened by a nearby predator or snake? Sometime later when the horse had wandered back to its barn with pieces of the buggy harness dragging behind, a search party was organized and they soon found the overturned buggy and the body. He had been thrown into a tree and sustained several broken bones including his neck.

With no family to see to his burial he was laid next to Levi Beardsley on the McVean property. Most of the hamlet's residents attended the burial. It was generally felt that he would be greatly missed.

Not that he had possessed any great medical skills, he was competent at setting bones and doing amputations. He was proficient at sewing up the many gashes and other wounds that accompany pioneer life, the poultices used on these repairs did more good than was generally understood. For these are dark days in American medical history and there is little that can be done medically for most maladies or injuries of a serious nature. In fact it's not a bad idea to steer clear of many who professed to be medical doctors as their bleedings and use of leeches do little to help the afflicted.

The doctor here had been more a moral booster and competent mid-wife than a curer of the sick. During these times the use of herbs and relying on your body to overcome and heal your afflictions was the best choice.

This unfortunate death occurred in late November and the community immediately sent inquiries for a replacement but as Winter settled in hard no taker showed. What birthing took place, and it seemed that a woman somewhere was giving birth every couple of weeks, was attended to by the experienced mid-wives around.

The first case shows up in the school. One of the seven year old girls has a fever so Bertha and Ann made her comfortable on the bear skin and send one of the older boys for her parents. Her father soon comes and picks the child up. Her fever still rising, Bertha and Ann have applied damp cloths to help keep it down.

By the middle of the week following, several children are absent and several of those that do show up show signs of being ill. Coughing and low fevers seemed common so Bertha decides to close the school. Word soon spreads that most of the children living south of the river have measles. By the end of two weeks nearly every child under fifteen is ill. The first girl has recovered and seems fine.

Bertha begins to show symptoms and takes to bed, she has heard of the problems associated with being pregnant and catching measles. She wants to have a healthy baby so bad. Ann, on the other hand says that she had had measles when she was twelve and stays healthy. Little Katherine develops a mild fever but in a few days seems fine.

By the end of three weeks the localized epidemic seems past and after another week Bertha is up and about, Ann having seen the Boyle children through their illness. As people begin moving about among the homes south of the river word comes that two small children not yet of school age had died along with a six year old girl who had sat next to the first case in Bertha's school.

It is not unusual to have these little epidemics go through portions of a community. The occurrence of such outbreaks are taken in stride by early settlers.

Reconvening classes, Bertha and Ann return the school to its normal routine. After a few days Bertha complains of a discomfort in her lower abdomen. Ann immediately gets her to go home, dismisses the school and follows Bertha up the mountain road. She catches up to the ill headmistress and helps her on home. Soon Richard appears, alerted by one of the older children at Ann's direction.

All that Ann and Richard can do is try to keep Bertha comfortable. She professes to feel better after being in bed awhile. When she starts to hemorrhaging Ann has Richard go after the woman who had mid-wifed for her Katherine.

Bertha knows she is spontaneously aborting and is very upset with the turn of events. Ann doing everything she can to help her is mostly concerned about stopping the bleeding once the fetus has passed. Once the neighbor woman arrives she looks the situation over and in conference with Richard and Ann, says there is little that can be done but stopping the bleeding.

By evening time it is evident that the bleeding has lessened. At the woman's insistence and with her assistance, Bertha has made an effort to expel any remaining tissue and now they settle down to a watchful routine. By full dark the bleeding has stopped, Ann and the neighbor woman have clean up and removed any sign of what has happened. Bertha has settled into a much needed deep sleep. Richard says that he will keep watch and sends Ann and the neighbor woman home to their families with his heartfelt thanks.

Dozing in a chair at her bedside, Richard is awakened by a touch at his hand. As his eyes focus on her, he sees that she has come full awake and is smiling wanly, at him.

Having been very fearful that he might lose her, he takes her up in his arms in a great hug of thanksgiving. It is obvious that her body has survived but her spirit is much depressed by the loss of the child. Over the next few days she begins to move about the home and is often seen staring out a window seemingly lost in thought.

Chapter Four
Wandering Souls

During the months that Ann has been helping and working with Bertha they have gradually developed a close personal relationship, one in which each feels that she can confide in the other personal thoughts that are not shared with their husbands. The friendship and confidence in a peer has given Bertha something that until now has not been available to her. With no sister and having changed homes just when most young females are bonding with other females of their same age, Bertha has had to rely upon her own inner strength and prolific writing in her diary to 'feel' her way through the situations that life has brought. Her marriage to Richard had opened new avenues of thought for her but she has found that male ego and considerations of a woman's 'place' often preclude open discussion of many of her concerns.

Under these circumstances it seems natural that she seeks out Ann to discuss her feelings about losing the baby and where she wishes to direct her life. She knows that Richard would be offended and hurt by some of what she is thinking. She is unsure that her arguments could change or ease his concerns. Dealing with the male ego is quite new to her, something she is working her way through.

As the long winter nights have given way to longer warmer days and the snows have disappeared from even the shaded spots in the forest, the various members of the Boyle/Jewell family have begun moving about the mountain property and the valley area in pursuit of various goals.

Richard is busy catching up on business activities precluded by the winter's cold and snows. David has begun mapping the area in anticipation of an intense search for the rumored mine. Bertha has begun to take long walks up the mountain by herself in quiet contemplation, having forgotten how much she had enjoyed this kind of activity as a young teenager.

While the Boyle/Jewell family has thrown off the shackles of winter so have the other residents of the area.

Ron Baldwin

Jane and Samuel are seen making the trip down to the river and back with her husband as he goes to work. She is beginning to show signs of mid-stage pregnancy. Her husband William, and Ann's husband Henry, often share the boat that now ferries them and other workers to the Susquehanna's north side and back. Jane uses the opportunities to flirt with the other men gathered at the boat landing. William is glad to have a wife that other men find amusing and puts no thought into any possibility of infidelity, they have had a renewing of sexual activity every since learning of his new job. He has no thought of her continual need of male attention.

On the morning that he has to leave for two or more days to do surveys on the upper Otsdawa he thinks nothing of it when Jane makes loud reference to him being gone two days as they part at the boat landing. Others are not as nearly unobservant.

Late that afternoon, when Henry crosses the river he is accompanied by two other mill workers who have spoken of a need to get home early. As Henry heads up the mountain the other two appear to turn toward their homes up river. Once out of sight they take to the forest and set a path toward the little cluster of homes near Bertha's school. Henry arrives home and turns his attention to Katherine as Ann prepares the evening meal. The Boyle children have climbed the road past the Ward cabin when the two men slip from the trees and approach the cabin from the rear. Well aware of the story circulating about, involving Jane and Jonah and not wishing to cross paths with Richard, the two men are very cautious in their approach while becoming excited about what they are about to enjoy.

Slipping up to the back door one of the men remains behind the woodshed as the other softly taps at the door. Jane, hopeful that her message has been received, hears the tapping and quietly opens the door a crack. She sees a young man she recognizes and smiles broadly.

"Let me ge' rid of the kid," she implores turning to Samuel and telling him, "Ge' in the yard 'til I call for ya'." Knowing that tone of voice the child hustles out the front door. He has become quite adept at entertaining himself for hours at a time.

Then she pulls the back door fully open for the young man, not seeing that another is lurking in the shadows. Fairly leaping into the man's arms she makes him welcome by pressing her charms to him. He quickly gives in to the moment and they both begin pulling at the other's clothing. With them both half naked the back door swings open and a grinning man stands taking in the scene. "'urry up kid," he directs to the young man, "Or ge' out th' way and let a man show you how!"

At first taken aback, Jane pulls her clothing over her exposed breasts. This was more than she had bargained for!

Then seeing the looks of lust on both faces she quickly thinks to control the situation. "Nobody need be in a 'urry," she allows softly, "Relax and enjoy." The two males look at each other and grin a knowing and understanding grin. She lets the clothes covering her breasts fall away while both men look on appreciatively.

"First you," she indicates to the younger one, "Then you," she states to the older man. And lest they get anxious, she murmurs, "we h've all night."

Night descends upon the little group of homes as Samuel plays under twinkling stars, the silence only broken by a distant wolf howling and an owl hooting from a nearby tree.

Down at the Martins they have shared the evening meal and set talking of Katherine and their future. Gone for the moment, anyway, Henry's need for hard drink, as his family pushes his past hurts far into his subconscious.

Up at the Boyle/Jewell home Bertha has finished the plans for the next day's classes and she and Richard have a few quiet moments alone, the three children having been sent off to bed.

"What if we never have children?" she asks of Richard.

Caught off guard and not sure how to reply, Richard stares into the fire and contemplates his answer. Thinking him reluctant to speak his mind, she reminds him of his obligation to be frank.

Still looking at the flames and nodding that he understands, he begins, "I have always wanted children and still do. When I knew that I wanted to marry you I was aware that my desires had to be balanced with yours. I do not believe that this miscarriage is anything but bad luck and not a warning of the future."

"Richard, I want you to know that right now I'm too scared to take another chance. I love you very much but I can not contemplate going through a miscarriage again."

"Well then, I would say that we must give things some time. I am sure that you will get through this."

"Don't be too sure," she says rising to go to bed.

Once in bed where they had always snuggled close each night, at the very least, she turns to her side and settles down as a tear slips onto her pillow. "How to make him see her side?" slides across her mind as she drops off to sleep.

Down the hallway David has struggled to fall asleep. Not having the recurrent nightmares anymore about his parents perishing, he nonetheless finds it difficult to slip off to sleep and tonight with that wolf howling somewhere out there, reminds him of that night, he and his siblings had huddled under blankets next to their dying mother, hearing a distant wolf howling. Living where the tragedy had happened does not seem to cause him problems. That ride up the hill when he returned, had been a terrible test. All the way up his stomach had knotted and a great anxiety had welled up in his mind, but upon seeing the house restored and the yard cleaned up he had quickly settled down. It seems to be the long deep dark nights and the occasional night sound that resurrect the terror.

Up along the Otsdawa Creek, William has made camp for the night. A nearby wolf answers one far off down the valley only to be challenged by that of a panther. That yowl silences the wolves but reminds William that he must remain cautious in his wanderings. He reaches and throws a couple more chunks of wood on the fire.

Bertha

Early morning light finds the two adventuring men making their way toward their respective homes, the younger one, unmarried, shrugs off his family's questioning looks. The older married man, boldly strides in demanding his breakfast while his much abused wife cowers over the cook stove. She knows what he has done and can only guess with whom. She marks the day in her memory and scraps some eggs and meat onto a plate which she sets before him with a cup of hot tea. A wee smile crosses her face as he drinks deeply.

A few days later he has taken to bed, a 'mysterious' ailment that caused his limbs to become cold and his breathing to become ragged. His wife had continued to watch over him giving him warm tea to help the chills. When he breathed his last rasping breath she had smiled and dumped the remaining tea outside and rinsed the pot thoroughly. A neighbor came and dug his grave, the widow and his children watched as the dirt was thrown back over him. They went on with their lives, she eventually remarries.

Up at the Ward cabin Jane has admonished Samuel to not tell his father of the long night spent in the yard and curled up in the woodshed for shelter from the cold and dampness. He was awakened at dawn by the sounds of the two men leaving.

"I'll be back," he had heard the younger one state.

"Come along before we're seen," an older gruffer voice had commanded. There is the sound of two people embracing, then the door closing and on looking out, all Samuel sees is the receding backs of his mother's visitors. Inside Jane hustles about freshening the bed and cleaning up any evidence of her indiscretions. That evening when William returns, Samuel is playing gleefully by the fireplace and his wife greets him, most cheerfully.

What one believes to be a secret is anything but, when more that one knows of it. Secrets in small communities are often the most well known commodities.

Bertha having heard rumors of herbs that will keep a woman childless, begins to look into the possibilities. That this kind of knowledge is known to rest with the Indians, she begins to inquire as to where one might find an Indian with such knowledge.

Few Indians are seen moving about on the old hunting trails and only stories of occasional camps that move on as fast as they are noted, seem to be her link to what she seeks. One day an old hunter from up river, stops by the school, having heard that she seeks knowledge of local Indians. Once she apprises him of her interest in herbs he offers to guide her to a small encampment near the mouth of the Charlotte Creek. Bertha agrees to ride up river the following Saturday to where he will be waiting for her.

At the appointed time she fords the mouth of the Charlotte Creek where he is waiting beside the trail. "We will have to leave the horses here," he says, "We will have to proceed on foot." He leads off into the thick hemlock forest rising above them. "Be watchful, there are rattlesnakes about."

For an hour or more, they climb through nearly impenetrable forest until at last they climb around a rocky cliff and come out on level ground covered with magnificent hardwood trees towering above them. A few strides in this more open and airy woodlands and two young Indians appear, one each side of them. Her guide does not seem alarmed, while Bertha is somewhat taken back by their sudden appearance.

The hunter and the two exchange greetings, while both young men stare appreciatively at Bertha, it is obvious that they are struck by her beauty. She stands proud and is not unmoved by their youthful good looks. Once they understand her reason for being here they point in the direction they should go. One leads, the old man then Bertha following, with the second bringing up the rear, close enough that he can smell her freshness. While his nearness causes her concern she is sure the old man would not lead her into trouble. She smiles back at the youth who grins, broadly.

Soon they work their way down a wide draw and come upon several circular shelters grouped in a rough circle, a small stream nearby. The approach of the two whites has invoked much curiosity and all in the encampment have gathered around to see. The old hunter, with a mixture of hand signs, Dutch, English and Indian words conveys that Bertha desires to know of the herbs they use. This brings two elderly women to the forefront who then indicates that she should accompany them. The old hunter nods his assurances and Bertha finds herself in one of the shelters where the women bring forth many small bags of skin containing various dried herbs. As best he can, the hunter interprets a name and use for each, these being indicated by touching and rubbing various parts of their body. Bertha is making some written notes and her scribbling are an object of curiosity.

Believing that she has learned what she has intended, Bertha continues to make notes, realizing that she is being exposed to hundreds of years of knowledge. As gifts she writes her name on several pieces of paper and hands them to the helpful women. They indicate their gratitude then the two young men accompany them back to the edge of the mountain. Before making the descent Bertha notes that they can see for miles westward down the valley below.

Back at the horses Bertha thanks her guide and invites him to come to dinner soon. Before they part he asks that she not speak about where he has taken her as these Indians mean no one harm and he considers them his friends. She agrees to remain silent. She also determines to return for the purpose of teaching them to write.

Having learned that here in the springtime is the best time to gather fresh herbs Bertha asks her guide to show her and Ann where to find the herbs on the mountain back of her home. He agrees to do this the following day, good weather prevailing. If not, then the following Saturday.

On the ride home Bertha stops by Ann's to tell her of the chance to learn of the herbs and where to gather them. They set plans to meet at Bertha's in the morning.

Richard, assuming that the two women only want to expand their knowledge and being very busy himself approves that they will be accompanied by the old hunter, a man he knows well by reputation. The project on the upper

Otsdawa is coming together and he and William have set Sunday to transfer the survey information to a set of maps prior to completing the sale.

The next morning finds the two women dressed for an excursion into the forest when their guide shows up. He points out that to do this it is best they go afoot. To gather herbs requires that the gatherer have an intimate knowledge of the subject plants, their appearances and habitats. The two women enjoy the wandering about and carry on a continuous conversation, much of which the old hunter ignores believing white women to be entirely too talkative. He much prefers the company of more stoic Indian females.

The pause at mid-day does bring him much joy though as he has little chance to consume the breads and pastries brought along for the purpose. He makes a point of setting the kitchens of these chatty two in his memory bank.

By early afternoon they have gathered and noted the locations of many herbs. Laying them out on a flat rock, Bertha has him go over them each so that both women know them well and their uses. She then sends him on his way, wanting to use this opportunity to talk with Ann. The last of the bread and pastries are passed to him and he departs to quieter places.

As she and Ann gather each herb into its own container, Bertha asks, "Do you intend to have more children?"

"With Henry's enthusiasm for the marriage bed I expect there will be many more."

"But do you want more? It seems the women around us are perpetually pregnant and it obviously takes a great toll on their health."

"My mother told me it was a woman's duty to accommodate her husband. And I can see that by doing that children are to be expected."

"Yes, but what if you could accommodate him and avoid pregnancy?"

"My religious training says it is my duty to 'go forth and be fruitful'."

"Yes, but shouldn't we have a choice as to 'how fruitful'?"

"Bert you speak of things that are outside of our society's normal accepted ways."

"But why are they 'acceptable'? Because a man says so, or a minister teaches it? What about our right to make choices? The Declaration of Independence says that, 'all men are created equal' and I believe that extends to us females as well!"

"Bert you fill my head with strange thoughts that I fear will not improve my marriage. To an extent, I know that I can get pregnant if I am with my husband on certain days each month. I admit to you that I try very hard to avoid being with him during those days. But it is very hard sometimes to turn him down. Just last month I thought we had crossed the line and I have prayed, apparently successfully, that I be spared this time. But what is a woman to do?"

"Certainly not feel she has to accept all pregnancies just because they are possible. I understand and feel the need and obligation to perpetuate a family but I question how many children need to be born to accomplish this."

"My head spins with all this. Where do you intend to take this?"

"Not one word to Richard or Henry I implore you. None of what we share about this need get out. One of the herbs we gathered today is used by the Indians to assure infertility. I will share that knowledge with you later if you ask. Now let's gather some strawberries to make tarts. They used to be abundant in the draw where the creek starts near my house."

Glad to have the subject changed, Ann smiles, "A good idea!" And the two head off out through the trees hand in hand.

Bertha carefully dries and stores, properly labeled, the herbs she and Ann have accumulated. Sure in her own mind of what she wants, she begins using the infertility herbs. Realizing no side effects she is determined to continue their use.

The months go by in rapid succession, Jane has a baby girl she names Polly and life on the upper Susquehanna has a regularity that seems to breed complacency. William and Richard are busy with work and training the new man. Bertha has convened school for the summer session and attendance is regular.

While Jane had continued to 'entertain' the pregnancy soon turned her suitors off and she has worked on her relationship with William since the birth. One of those perpetually thin women, her body has quickly thrown off most signs of childbearing.

Bertha has returned to the Indian encampment and offered, through her guide, to teach those that want to learn English and how to write. It was arranged that every Saturday morning a group of them are to meet her by the Charlotte Creek ford and now, months later, she is seeing some real results.

Sticking close to her 'cycle' she has again returned to having relations with Richard who doesn't complain about the infrequency. It is evident that he wishes to work with her instead of pushing his 'husband's rights'.

The next three years go by with little change. Then a family named McDonald arrives in 1805, and purchases the McVean mills and a parcel of land along the lower Silver Creek. Soon they have dismantled and moved the mills to new locations on the creek. Here the ice and spring floods will do minimal damage and the mills should be operational year-round. Over the ensuing months the center of activity of the hamlet slowly changes from the old mill sites to McDonald's location. With more and more farmers coming to the mills to grind their grains or saw their lumber other tradesmen and craftsmen set up shop nearby. The gathering of businesses and residences soon becomes known as McDonalds Mills to those living around the area.

During the same time frame other communities up and down the Susquehanna Valley are developing. Only time and events will determine which like Cooperstown, Cherry Valley, Oneonta and Sidney will prevail and which like the area on the upper Oneonta Creek and the upper

Bertha

Otsdawa Creek, both with viable fast growing populations in 1806, will gradually decline into obscurity. Encouraged by the State legislature, private companies are building better roads connecting the upper Susquehanna Valley to other areas of the state. Where these roads start, terminate or pass through often will determine the chances of that community to grow and prosper.

With change come new opportunities and failures. The predominate farming of Otsego County is in perpetual flux. Grain farming gradually is giving way to sheep and beef which eventually will give way to dairying. As this process proceeds the tradesmen and craftsmen come and go with the trends. The overall population of the area continues to grow while the names change as property owners come and go. The land sales and surveying businesses remains a stable form of employment.

Richard and William had been uncontested in their work except where their interests had bumped up against the Coopers or the Morris'. Just after the sale of the McVean mills another land office opens up in the hamlet. Because William and the Houghtaling boy, Elihu, are the best and most experienced surveyors in the area, they are called on by the new land office to perform surveys. Richard is just as happy to let them take over that part of his business completely, the selling and promoting of land taking up most of his time.

On June 16th of 1806, an unusual astrological occurrence is made note of in most every journal and diary of the times. A rare full eclipse of the sun began about 9:50 AM and ended about two hours later. So complete was the darkness that the chickens went to roost and night birds could be heard in the woods.

Each summer with the school closed Bertha has taken to making trips to Boston of New York for the main purpose of improving her library and what she can offer her students. This the summer of 1806 she has convinced Henry to allow Ann to accompany her. They have gone by coach from Cooperstown on the newly built Second Great Western Turnpike to Cherry Valley and on to Albany then from there by schooner down the Hudson. Arriving in the city they take rooms at the oft used, by travelers from the north, boardinghouse of Mary Daubeny on Wall Street. Here they cross paths with Judge Cooper and his son Richard, in town on business. The men invite Bertha and Ann to share their table that evening and the two women accept.

The dinner conversation centers on developments back home and Bertha's school. The two women are introduced to several other visitors and local business men. When the little group breaks up and heads for their respective rooms, the women agree to join the Judge and Richard for breakfast.

Ann, who has never had the opportunity to socialize with landed and educated gentlemen is quite taken with the Coopers. "They seem to have a good grasp of the situations we face back home," she remarks to Bertha.

"Richard has told me that much of what the Judge has accomplished has been because of his closeness to his settlers. But, that in his haste, he has made many mistakes. Poor surveying of tracts has caused many problems."

"Mr. Richard Cooper has a more gentlemanly air about him while his father often speaks rather crudely," Ann observes.

"I believe his son has been schooled at a university and I find it interesting that you make such a distinction. When you began working with me in the school you too used many of the terms the Judge uses. That you have learned so much yourself makes me proud."

"Oh Bert, you fill my head with your compliments!"

"Be proud of yourself! Being able to converse with learned persons should be a thing of pride."

"Already I look forward to breakfast!" gushes Ann.

"As do I," murmurs Bertha, "Now please settle down and get some sleep, we have a busy day ahead of us."

Breakfast finds Mrs. Daubeny's dining room fairly bustling with activity as businessmen and others join up with travelers to commence the day. The Coopers are already seated when the women enter the room. The buzz of conversations dims perceptibly as nearly every male set of eyes watch the two approach the Judge's table. The two men arise and bow to them as they are seated. As quickly a seemingly steady stream of men have business with the Judge and walk away shaking their heads when they learn that the Judge's two lovely companions are married.

One young man, introduced as the son of the man talking to Judge Cooper, recently graduated from Yale law school, holds Bertha's hand noticeably longer that the occasion would call for while he looks deeply into her eyes. He kisses the back of her hand gently, while giving it a more than gentlemanly squeeze. He smiles as he releases her hand and sees the blush of heat cause her bosom to heave and redden her cheeks. "Perhaps there is some way I might be of service to you. I have time as I am awaiting several interviews with prospective employers."

Still trying to gain her composure Bertha, hesitates her answer. Ann quickly spouts, while he is greeting her, "How gracious! Bert this solves our dilemma of an escort. Do say yes!"

Put in that position, Bertha allows that having a knowledgeable guide would hasten the search for bookstores so she acquiesces, "Perhaps you could be of service, young man," she pointedly says. She can see that he gets the message but hardly believes he is deterred.

"I will acquire us a coach," he offers and as quickly is out the door.

Ann smiles at Bertha who gives her a look meant to convey, "Rein yourself in."

Nevertheless, Ann holds onto her enthusiasm. The whole prospect of moving about this great city and learning of its charms has her nearly giddy with the prospects.

By the end of the day Bertha is glad for his help and guidance. They have made arrangements for several cases of books to be shipped home. Returning them to the boardinghouse, the young lawyer asks if he can accompany them at the evening meal. For the moment, forgetting his earlier impertinence Bertha accepts then she and Ann retire to their room to freshen up.

"That was great!" shouts Ann, "I have never seen so many people so busy in all my life!"

"A bit more so than Boston," Bertha replies.

"Young Edward was very helpful and gracious," Ann testifies.

"Did you note how he greeted me this morning?" Bertha inquiries of her friend.

"Why no, whatever do you mean?"

"He was very impertinent in the way he squeezed and kissed my hand. Yet, I must admit I found it rather exciting!"

"I thought him very gentlemanly. Do you think he wished you to get a different message?"

"Implicitly."

"Then why have dinner with him? Are you tempted to see how far he will go?" Ann inquires reprovingly.

"Certainly not! But I am hoping we have a conversation that is not about land and farming!"

"That would be interesting. I will watch, if he gets impertinent I will help you withdraw."

"And if he decides to flirt with you, should I interfere or not?" Bertha asks, with a sense of humor in her voice.

"Oh Bert, no man is going to turn from you to me!"

"Don't underestimate yourself, Ann. You are a very pretty woman and your new found assurance makes you very attractive. Let's go down for dinner and Mr. Edward Craft had better watch out!" They both giggle as they depart the room.

At dinner Mr. Craft seems more interested in the prospects back at McDonald's Mills than giving either woman his attentions, separately. By the time the meal is finished he has garnered himself an invitation to visit the hamlet as a guest of the Jewells and to escort the two women the next day on a clothes hunting expedition. The Youngs' store doesn't fully meet Bertha's clothing selection desires and she wishes to outfit Ann in some finer dresses than she has been used to wearing. She has plans to outfit Nancy and the two boys in the latest styles as well.

Bertha

Driving the two women around the streets of New York City gives young Craft a chance to interrogate them further about the needs for a lawyer in McDonald's Mills. While his father wishes him to join a New York City firm, Edward, as a result of these conversations, has come to realize that by accepting little now he may be able to build his own practice in this small frontier community. By the time he has again returned them to the boardinghouse he has made up his mind.

Asking to set with them a moment before they part company he surprises them with an apology. "Mrs. Jewell, I feel that I should apologize for my atrocious behavior the morning we met. I fear that I acted much as big city men tend to act toward 'county cousins'. There is no excuse for my impertinence, and I beg your forgiveness."

"I find it refreshing that you recognize your mistake and take no offense at your actions," Bertha rejoins, "For two days you have more than made up for your mistake. We are not offended and will look forward to seeing you back home."

"That is much of why I desired this conversation, as I have decided to try my fortunes in this McDonald's Mills and ask if it would be all right if I accompany you both back there?"

Looking at Ann, who obviously likes the idea, Bertha says, "We would be delighted for your company, I'm sure you can help breakup an otherwise boring long sail up the Hudson. I know that my husband will be delighted that we have brought home an honest lawyer." She remarks with a little obvious humor. And to herself she thinks, "It will be nice to have an educated person as a friend. And having his youthful good looks around won't hurt either."

Arriving back home the two women are greeted by husbands tired of their own cooking and child watching. That the women have such an educated well spoken young man in tow only causes Henry troubled thoughts until Ann gets him to bed, then all concerns fall away. In the back of his mind, Richard also has his concerns but knowing Bertha, he is not surprised. Even when she insists on putting Edward up until he can make more permanent arrangements, he finds no reason to do otherwise.

And so another year makes its way toward conclusion while the area residents struggle to establish themselves. The Fall sees a good many rafts of lumber, sawn during the summer, leave for the Chesapeake Bay. During that winter, the McDonalds and other mill owners pile large piles of lumber in preparation for the spring rafting which is a much larger undertaking. The lumber is built into 'cribs' which are lashed together with mast quality pines, the whole affair often reaching 100 feet in length. Shallow boats are built and sealed with pine pitch to keep water from seeping to the hogsheads packed with grains, potatoes, maple sugar and other commodities that are piled high on them. Cribs of lumber are lashed to the sides and this makes up other rafts that are lashed together in preparation of spring thaw. Once the ice goes out, which lowers the many rafts into the water, crews set about guiding them with the current down river. Because so many locations along the Susquehanna and its tributaries have mills on them there is a great migration on the river all at the same time, in order to catch the spring floods. For days rafts are seen moving along the river toward the New York and Pennsylvania border. Most of the rafters are well experienced on the river and make the trip down only to walk all the way back. For many of the young men of the upper Susquehanna this presents a chance at great adventure, few have not ridden a raft to Baltimore and walked back.

Having been responsible for sawing much of the lumber for the McDonalds and never having taken a raft down river, this year Henry Martin decides is his year to go. So as the days warmed and the river rose he, like the others, began packing food and clothing to last the four or five weeks the round trip would take. Assigned to a raft with an experienced crew he is well versed in his duties for the trip. Before the ice goes out a steady rain begins falling and the crews are called to their rafts as it appears that the river will open suddenly. They sleep on the rafts that night and early the next morning the ice and rafts all begin moving at once.

Immediately the men are busy pushing ice floes away and steering the rafts into the deepest currents. At the Otego Creek the flow greatly increases and several other rafts join the run. At times like these smaller rafts will lash along side other rafts and the combined crews can better control things. As the McDonald rafts approach the confluence with the Unadilla River the lead oarsman yells out a warning. The waters of the two rivers have formed a whirlpool that now holds two smaller rafts in its swirling grip. The much larger McDonald raft is headed straight for the smaller ones at an alarming rate. The crew struggles to turn the massive raft and succeed in missing one while taking the second broadside. The collision throws all on board both rafts to their knees that had sense enough to grab something solid. As they all righted themselves, the two rafts separate and slip clear of the whirlpool. The foreman of the McDonald raft takes a quick head count and comes up one short. "Anybody seen Henry!" he calls out and all begin casting their eyes about the river of swirling water and ice floes.

At one point a crewman thought he saw an armed raised above the surface but in the end they had to conclude that he was gone. Each year the river claimed a toll for using its powerful flow.

Back at McDonald's Mills, Ann would not get the word for another month, not until the first of the crews straggle back to town. The bearer of bad news found her at the school with Bertha and when Ann saw his face she knew the worst had happened. She lets out a long wail, "No!" collapsing at his feet.

Bertha immediately sends the children home, drawing young Katherine to her as the crewman helps get Ann to the house, a short distance from the school. Ann is immediately put to bed and given a cup of tea from the leaves of Indian tobacco, an herb. Shortly she has regained some of her composure and can communicate with Bertha.

The crewman having been dispatched to get Richard, it isn't long when he arrives. Made aware of the tragedy by the messenger, he isn't surprised to see Ann barely able to talk. It is decided that Ann and Katherine should be taken to the Jewell home for a few days.

Henry's body was never found and with no body a funeral seemed unnecessary. Several couples made the trek up the mountain to deliver their condolences but otherwise life in McDonald's Mills went on. Ann soon removes herself and Katherine back to their home and returns to working with Bertha at the school. It being close to planting time they are preparing to close school until mid-summer.

Chapter Five
Death Strikes

Life on the frontier was harsh and all to often, brief. Necessity caused people to do what, under other circumstances, they would hardly even contemplate.

Ann, obviously torn by the loss of her husband, throws herself into reading all the books Bertha has been able to accumulate, along with spending long hours with Katherine, now 6.

While at the Jewell home getting her mind settled she and lawyer Craft had had the opportunity to talk casually on several occasions. She could see that while a few years her junior, he had ambition and was intent on building a position in life.

In a few weeks after Ann and the child have moved back home he comes calling, Ann makes him welcome with tea and pastries. The next day he comes with a buggy and takes Ann and Katherine up the mountain on a picnic near the springs that provide the Jewells and other homes below, with cool, clear water. It being springtime the anemones and lady-slippers are in bloom, overhead the basswood and chestnut trees are covered with flowers abuzz with honeybees, while scattered through the forest dogwoods spread their springtime splendor. The couple set watching Katherine play among the flowers and catching the occasional orange salamander from in under stones she turns.

Craft carefully leads the conversation to the fact that Ann has a child to rear and no husband to help provide. He pointedly avoids mentioning that he needs to find housing away from the Jewells'. Slowly he works his comments around to the possibility that he be looked upon as a suitor.

Ann, having anticipated where he was headed and mindful of her situation had already convinced herself that if he asked, she would accept. She knows that there is no love, but has thoughts that with time she could come to love him.

To her it is evident that he doesn't yet love her but is very considerate of her thoughts and position. He has told himself that this is the practical way to solve both their problems and that she is certainly desirable enough that he would enjoy sharing her bed.

By the time the warm afternoon has worn down they have come to an understanding. He has taken her hand and they have wandered among the towering hardwoods, Katherine scurrying about their feet. Pausing at one point, he draws her to him and they kiss. Responding to his embrace she presses to him and he feels his passions rise. Stepping back he says, "We should go to the Jewells' and tell them of our intentions. I would like to know that they sanction our union."

Pleased that he would want her friend's approval, Ann smiles, "By all means. Can we go directly?"

"I'll get the buggy."

It is only a short ride to the Jewell home. Bertha is reading on the front porch enjoying the warm spring day and view of the valley below. When the buggy approaches from in the direction of the springs she feels that something has happened. The smiles on their faces give them away.

"You two seem in high spirits!" she exclaims as they climb down, partially anticipating the reason for this mid-afternoon visit, "Come, set with me and tell me your news."

Once she is told of the decision to marry, Bertha embraces Ann enthusiastically while whispering in her ear, "We must talk."

"I love spring weddings," Bertha says, "I insist that it be here."

Edward is delighted to see the acceptance of what he knows is mostly a 'relationship of convenience'. But he can't stop thinking about the promise of that kiss and embrace. Ann is obviously a passionate as well as beautiful woman and this 'liaison' may hold more than he had hoped for.

It is quickly determined that the wedding should take place in two weeks here in the yard, weather allowing. Bertha wants to make a big thing of it both as a way to celebrate with her friend and to introduce Edward to the community at large.

The two friends agree that Ann will use the dress that Bertha was married in. That they would send for Judge Cooper to perform the ceremony and invite the Cooper family to attend.

The appointed Sunday arrives with a warm sun and soft breeze. Richard is afforded the honor of escorting the bride. Judge Cooper performs the ceremony and partakes of the refreshments then he and his son Richard and his wife take their leave and start the long journey home.

Richard and Bertha stand on the porch saying 'good-byes' to the departing guests. They both are pleased with the fact that they have assumed the position of community leaders. Long after the newly-weds have taken a buggy down to their new home, the hosts stand arms around each other taking in the view as the shadows of a setting sun slowly creep across the valley and up the hill sides.

Down below, an expectant bride slips from her wedding dress to the appreciative look of her new husband. Once she is free of it and the brassiere he commences to undress. It is obvious that both will enjoy this night.

Having had Katherine stay with them, Bertha takes her to Nancy's room and tucks the two girls in together. Then she checks on David and Charles both of which have had a fine day with other youths in attendance.

David at 15 had participated in a few dances with a couple of the local girls but his mind had remained on his quest, to find the rumored mine or disprove its existence. Over the past several years he has explored Panther Mountain from near the Charlotte Creek to across from the Otego Creek to its top and beyond, finding many places where rocky cliffs allowed examination of the under laying rocks. But his treks had failed to find a single trace of minerals that could be mined. The whole area seems to be consisting of flat rock, laid down eons ago under an ancient ocean. Some of the books Bertha had at the school have explained this process so that he understands it. The collection of fossil rocks, in his room, gives moot testimony to the area's wet past.

Above the Houghtaling place he found a cave that has been home to various animals over the years but it did not extend more than twenty feet or so into a cliff surrounded by a grove of tall white pines.

This last Fall he had discovered where his father had built the lean-to and left supplies against an Indian raid. The leather pouches had long rotted away and the wood of a pistol's stock had been chewed by rodents until about all that was left was the flintlock mechanism now too rusted to operate. He had added this to his collection of artifacts which includes a pan he had found where Isaac had built his shelter and items he has found lying about Sarah's grave. These last obviously of Indian origin.

Two more areas must be explored he has determined to be able to put the rumor of a mine to rest. One he can see every morning straight across the valley, the other is the steep slope across the Charlotte Creek that Bertha had climbed to meet the Indians living on top.

With school now dismissed for planting time David has the opportunity to plan expeditions to both sites. Telling Bertha of his plans she admonishes him to not ascend the ridge beyond the Charlotte alone, with out telling him of the Indians there. She has long lost her fear of his getting lost in these vast forests, having manifested his father's natural ability to wander fearlessly about the wilderness.

To allay her concerns he says that he will cross the river and explore the cliffs visible from their home, the ones that their father had called, 'Oneonta'. As usual he packs a little pemmican and johnny-cake and heads out early. The river is still up so he utilizes the work boat for a crossing though it adds a lot to the distance walks. The cliffs constitute a deeper cleft in the hill than others that he has explored. Well down the hill he finds shale, a rock that easily breaks up into smaller pieces. Up high he finds thicker sandstone much as he has found at the other cliffs in the area. Standing upon the summit he is treated to a somewhat different view than the one that had greeted his father and mother many years hence.

Across the valley the river sparkles its way as it skirts the mountain. The high ground, for the most part is covered with a verdant green forest while the valley floor is broken up into large fields of freshly plowed earth intermingled with the soft green of winter wheat sowed the previous fall. Off to his right a natural pond known as 'Pond Lilly' reflects the late morning sun surrounded with plowed fields. Here and there a man can be seen with a yoke of oxen or team of horses working up more soil. Way off down river a plumb of smoke marks where a settler is clearing land and creating potash in the process.

Lingering to take in the scene, much as his parents had done, David knows that there is no mine in this area, but he also knows that he won't be content until he has explored the high ridge east of the Charlotte. He makes plans to go there tomorrow hoping he can avoid Bertha at least until he has done what he has set out to do.

Standing on the porch in the late morning air, Bertha has seen her half-brother as he sat atop the cliffs opposite. It has given her pause to think about him and what drives him.

That night at dinner she changes her tack. "If you still wish to explore above the Charlotte I will go with you. We'll take a couple of horses then walk up, if you can deal with having company."

David has long ago learned not to oppose his half-sister when she has a plan. Besides, she has many times demonstrated that she can handle herself as well as most men. The idea of having company sets well so he agrees. They make plans to start early the next day.

Come morning finds them both with full packs saddling the horses. Richard bids them be careful and puts a pistol in Bertha's pack. They ride off together in high spirits and about an hour later tie the horses where they can reach some grass and head into the hemlock forest that skirts the ridge above them.

They have not gone far up the ridge when David spots some shale outcroppings much like below 'Oneonta'. He relates his findings to Bertha and continues to climb. Bertha follows not reveling that she has been here before. Reaching the final cliffs that rise to the top of the mountain, David again finds sandstone. Here there are huge chunks of it laying among the trees making the ascent more difficult and forcing them to climb among the rocks to reach the summit. Bertha's guide had known a clearer path up the ridge, but then he wasn't interested in what the ridge was made off.

Forging ahead David reaches above to pull himself up and just as he does, he feels the rattlesnake bite his arm. Immediately he releases his grip and slips down behind a boulder out of Bertha's sight.

Thinking that he has simply slipped and fallen she calls out, "Are you all right?" A long pause follows.

"Don't come up here Bert!" he calls out.

The tone of his voice warns her and at the same moment she remembers the old hunter's warning about rattlesnakes. Carefully climbing as close to him as she can, Bertha can see that he is setting with his back to a rock his legs stretched out of her sight. He is sucking at a bloody wound on his right fore arm. She can hear the distinct buzzing of several snakes.

Looking up he sees her there. "Don't come any closer, I don't know how many there are but there are several and I have been bitten on both legs as well as my arm."

Near panic herself, she is calmed by his demeanor. Remembering the pistol she retrieves it from the pack. Again getting as close as she can, she asks David if he can use his arms to drag himself to where she can get a hold of him.

"I'll try but my right arm is growing numb."

With no time to lose Bertha spots a stick and using it reaches to where David can grip it. She then says, "Don't move your legs, just let me drag you out of there."

Using her legs she pulls him partially from behind the rock. Reaching she grabs his arms and pulls him clear. A large rattlesnake that strikes at his receding foot gets a bullet for its efforts. She then, half pulling and half carrying gets him to a spot clear of rocks where she has him lay down and gets him a drink from her canteen.

As he continues to suck on his arm where he has obviously cut open the fang marks, she takes his knife and cuts up both breeches legs exposing the obvious fang marks on his right calf and left upper ankle.

Encounters with poisonous snakes, while not that common, were often enough so that most understood what had to be done. Each of David's obvious wounds probably wouldn't be fatal by themselves but multiple bites could very well kill him. Bertha is determined to avoid that if possible. Making cuts across both sets of fang marks she squeezes both attempting to increase the bleeding while he continues to suck on the arm wound and spit out the results. Bertha kneels where she can suck both leg wounds alternately. David continuing to suck and spit begins to grow weaker and finally lays back with a sigh.

Looking up from where she is kneeling Bertha knows that he is gone and now she can see that he had also been bit on his left neck, the venom apparently injected into an artery. He had never had a chance.

For a long time she remains kneeling, and as her father before had, wonders at all the needless death. Finally, with a stoic attitude of acceptance she stands up. Looking about so she is sure she can get back to this spot she descends and rides to the nearest homestead for help. A man and his son return with her and as they reach where the body lies they come upon the two Indians that had acted as guides on Bertha's first trek up this mountain, they said that they had come to investigate the shot and had found the white boy's body. They help cut saplings for a litter and assist in carrying the body down to the horses.

Bertha then rides home leading David's horse with him tied across the saddle. Nearing Ann's house, her friend comes out to learn what has happened. Richard is then sent for and shortly he, William and Edward are seen crossing the Susquehanna by boat. William and Edward get shovels and meet the little group at the Boyle cemetery just beyond the school house. In a couple of hours David is laid to rest beside his parents.

The following day, grief stricken and feeling guilty for having taken him there, Bertha writes to her uncles to let them know what has happened. She then informs Richard that she is going to Europe in a few weeks. She does this in a way that he knows he is not invited to accompany her. She then walks down to the Craft home and asks Ann to take Charles and Nancy while she is gone and to open the school for summer classes.

Ann offers to go with her but her offer is rejected. It is plain that Bertha wants some time alone to examine her life. Unable to convince her that she needs an escort, Ann agrees to take the children and to see to the summer classes, on the promise that Bertha would be back before cold weather.

Bertha has no expressed plans. She just knows that she has to get away and think for awhile. She has this feeling that her life is being driven by others and she has lost all control. Not that she doesn't love Richard, she knows he has been great with her, giving her latitude that other men of the times wouldn't even consider. That he had stayed by her side through the miscarriage and hasn't said a word about her lack of getting pregnant again means very much to her. Still something isn't right and she intends to figure out what it might be.

Chapter Six
Searching

Riding to Cooperstown, Bertha has left her horse with the Coopers and caught a stage to Albany via Cherry Valley. At Albany she has taken a room in an inn and has decided to spend a day or so thinking about where to go next. Europe had been a convenient destination that would guarantee that she wouldn't be expected back soon, "But where to go and how to solve the mystery of my future?" she has thought.

That evening at dinner by herself she has an experience that helps point her direction. Seated at a quiet corner table she was lost in thought when a man approached.

"Couldn't help but notice that you are eating alone. Waiting for someone or traveling alone?" he inquires.

Smiling up at him she is taken by his tall well dressed frame. Hesitating to answer, trying to decide between inviting him to join her and dismissing him for his impertinence, she takes in his rugged good looks marred only by a long scar on his right cheek, running from near the ear to his jaw bone. Obviously he had been badly cut by something or someone.

"Please pardon my forwardness Miss but I have a favor to ask should you be interested."

"Hm-m polite and good looking," she thinks, "Can't come to harm here."

"By all means, sir, set down and explain yourself," she says loud enough so nearby diners hear her. He bows and pulls out the chair to her left, giving him full view of the room with the wall to his back.

"You have nothing to fear from me," he offers softly leaning toward her as he speaks. The tone and demeanor designed to put her at ease.

She outwardly seems to relax her wariness and thinks, "Quite taken with his ability to manipulate." Smiling warily, Bertha keeps quiet while awaiting his explanations, her dark eyes looking deep into his watching for any sign of deceit.

"John Palmer, madam, I am a cattle buyer for the Army and in town to attend a local sale then on to Boston," he relates.

"And how does that relate to me?" she asks. Noting mentally, that he doesn't look like a cattleman.

"I thought you might be going that way and in need of an escort," he states.

"And you presume that I would allow a stranger to accompany me? How impertinent!" Raising her voice just enough to make the diners at the nearest table look around.

He reacts by raising his hand to her, palm down, as if to say, not so loud, please. The look on his face pleads his position as well.

Bertha instinctively knows that there is more than he has so far admitted to and her sense of adventure urges her to go along, for awhile. "Just how are we to present ourselves to other travelers should I accept?" she adventures.

"There is no need of presenting ourselves as anything other than what we are," he states, "I only offer to accompany you," he says looking away at that moment. "He's lying!" she thinks noting the furtiveness of his glance.

"I should end this now!" she warns herself.

"Mrs. Jewell I assure you that I have no ulterior motives," he lies. He knows he could use her as cover but can't bring himself to share his true motivations, at least not here in public. One never knows who is listening, or for whom.

She sets watching his eyes and trying to evaluate his interest in her, is it sexual? Does he think her 'available'? Surely he can see her wedding ring and he did address her as 'Mrs. Jewell' ? How did he know her name and why?

"Mr. Palmer, it is true that I travel alone on family business and can not imagine how I could gain by traveling as your companion, I am perfectly capable of taking care of myself."

"It would seem that my approach has upset you, for that I apologize and will withdraw immediately." He stands to depart. She looks on not sure why but is tempted to stop him.

Thinking better of it she says, "Your apology is accepted, Mr. Palmer." He bows and turning, heads for the lobby where he hesitates to see if she is moving or otherwise showing distress.

"We are not yet through with each other Mrs. Jewell", he thinks to himself, mounting the stairs to his room.

"What an interesting interlude," she thinks, "I wonder what his true motivation was?"

Next morning she has made up her mind and decided to go to Worcester to see her uncles and to take care of David's affairs. Waiting for a stage toward Boston she finds herself looking among the other travelers for Mr. Palmer. Strangely drawn to his physical presence she can't explain it to herself.

Since he is nowhere to be seen and the stage having arrived, she puts those thoughts aside and finds a seat by a window with another female by her side. She is soon lost in her own thoughts as the stage heaves and bounces along east. Arriving in Worcester she has a coach for hire take her to Charles'. Her Aunt Mary is elated to see her and soon has her settled in a spare room and has sent a messenger to Michael to inform him of her arrival and to invite them to supper.

Left to her own devices by Mary who goes to start the evening meal, Bertha unpacks a few things not really knowing how long she would linger. With a little time on her hands she writes a note to Richard to let him know where she is. There is no mention of the mystery of Mr. Palmer.

At supper she brings them all up to date on things along the Susquehanna as well as the circumstances of the tragic death of David. It has been months since the last letter had arrived from his son up the Otego Creek valley, so Charles is glad to hear of the crops growing situation in that area, knowing that his son's success or failure would depend on harvesting good crops.

Everyone is disturbed by David's death, he had been well liked while living with Charles and Mary. They all applaud her plan to have David's property and money transferred to Charles Michael and both uncles offer to accompany her to the bank and lawyer's offices on the morrow. She accepts and the party breaks up as Bertha says she needs some rest from the long, rough ride.

Getting the ownership transfers done lifts a burden from Bertha and now she feels free to attend to her own affairs. That evening she announces her desire to go on to Boston for her own reasons. Her uncles have assumed that Richard is quite busy with the land business and thus the reason for her coming this far alone, for her to go to Boston un-chaperoned is met with their resistance. They offer to have one of her aunts go along but she insists that she is safe alone. Privately she is thinking of sailing on to New York and who knows where after and does not want to have to explain her plans. She is properly thankful for the concerns and offers. Before leaving for Boston, Bertha wants to consult with Mr. Brindles about Charles Michael now owning the farm that had been Judith's parents place. He had expressed a desire to purchase the farm and now she wants to make him an offer that would finally sever any property ties here near Worcester.

Before leaving home she had talked with lawyer Craft about her finances as well as her brothers' and when she returns she intends to take proper care of the paperwork. The suddenness of the death of her brother has not only depressed her but made her pointedly aware of the obligations she has to others.

At the farm Bertha offers to sell Mr. Brindle the farm complete with all the animals and equipment at a price that makes him smile. Then she offers to hold the mortgage herself with a small interest rate and no money down. Knowing that this is more than fair he rides to town with her and they have the lawyer draw up the papers.

Bertha relieved to have struck a deal stops by the stage office and purchases a ticket for the morning trip. Only half aware of where she is going or why, she only knows that it feels right to be moving on. Giving thought to writing Richard and letting him know where she is headed, she decides instead to let him think her at Charles' for the time being.

Back at the school Ann has taken over the summer session and the students, mostly female, are doing well. Katherine is now one of the pupils as is Samuel, the Ward boy, Nancy and Charles Michael and ten other neighborhood children.

Edward has been pushing Ann to have another child but she has been using the herbs from Bertha and is determined to wait until she is fully settled within her new marriage.

When she had announced the intention to marry Edward Craft, Bertha had insisted that they discuss the implications fully. Ann had admitted to not having 'feelings' for him but the practical side of her could not turn away from the security of his offer. And yes, she did remember that it was Bertha he had tried to seduce. But he had acted as a complete gentleman since being rebuffed and so she didn't think he would stray. The two women had agreed that Ann should share the 'magic' herbs for the time being, until Ann was sure of the relationship. In the meantime Ann had found him to be an accomplished lover and she found herself looking forward to their frequent and often creative lovemaking.

For his part Edward Craft was also enjoying the lovemaking, finding Ann a pliant student of the finer art of it, while avoiding the obvious question, where did he learn such talents? He is just slick enough to have her thinking that they are discovering these 'secrets' together, and that the discoveries come out of a simple desire to please her.

Up the hill at the Wards cabin Jane has again become restless. The need to reward William for his success with Richard no longer motives her in bed. Each time she goes to the stores across the river she manages to pass rather slowly by the taverns where men are often lounging about.

Several of the locals have gotten the message implied. Talk has been bantered about concerning the possibilities and who would be first to take her up on the obvious offer. One of the men knows William personally and he speaks of disregarding her, that it would not be a good thing to cuckold a friend. Others held that he must not be doing the job of keeping her happy and they were sure that they could accomplish what he could not. Yet not one of them could bring himself to step forward and make Jane an offer. Talk remains talk and Jane grows restless.

One evening Edward Craft is enjoying his pipe on his porch when he sees Jane returning from her shopping. From a little distance her lithe body and bouncing hair presents a rather desirable picture. He watches her continue up the road, observing her strong, long legs at work and letting his mind wander and wonder where a married man should never be.

He had seen her before and knew that she and William lived in the cabin up the hill. Ann had shown no interest in the woman's existence so he had not given Jane further thought until this evening. Now in a moment of reverie he reverts to the man he was when he was back in the city and begins to plot an opportunity to get closer to Jane without alerting his wife. After all there might not be anything there, then again?

Jane had seen the puff of his smoke as she had turned up the hill. Knowing that taking long strides would show off her slim limbs she looked straight ahead, as if unaware of his presence, yet sneaking a sideward glance to assure herself of his interest. "One never knows from where comes the next big adventure," she thinks, "besides it would please her to entice the prim and proper Ms. Ann's husband. Serve her right!"

Ed finishes his pipe, knocks the ash out on the porch railing and returns inside. His mind rolling over various reasons to venture up the hill at the first opportunity.

Richard has kept busy while he and William continue to show and sell farms and parcels of land. He has received the letter from Bertha and feels secure in the knowledge that she is at her Uncle Charles'.

Bertha

Concluding her business in Boston, Bertha has taken passage on a packet boat to New York City and has arrived at Mrs. Daubeny's boardinghouse. Since walking down the gangway onto the New York wharf she has been aware that her eyes are watching for Mr. Palmer. This causes her some consternation as she is sure her interest is not of a personal nature but more of an adventurous hopefulness.

Settling into a room she thinks to take a stroll in the afternoon air. The boat ride had somewhat disturbed her stomach and she feels the need to give it time to settle before eating. A few minutes into her walk she finds herself strolling through a small park. As she, lost in her own thoughts, passes a bench under a huge oak tree a familiar voice reaches her.

"Mrs. Jewell, won't you set a moment?"

Startled out of her reverie she turns to the voice. "Why if it isn't the mysterious Mr. Palmer!"

Indicating that she should set beside him, he merely lowers his eyes from hers as he detects a certain tone of happy discovery in her voice. "Please," he says, sliding perceptibly back from where he has indicated she should set.

Feeling comfortable about the public setting and glad for the opportunity to explore her interests in this man she sets, hands clasped in her lap, and looks him in the eyes as if to say, so what now?

"If you will allow me, here in relative security of not being overheard I can tell you what I am about and why and how you might be of help," he offers, not explaining that an agent of his has been tailing her and reported her presence in the city. Thus the opportunity to set up this seeming casual meeting, out of ear shot and observance of others.

"I await your explanation," she says.

"If you have kept up with the news you know that this country is having problems with Great Britain. Just this past June they fired upon one of our ships as they continue to 'press' our sailors into service in their Navy. Some things resulting from our successful separation from them have continued to fester unresolved and because we have not yet asserted ourselves as a nation there are those that seek to feed unrest within the country. President Jefferson has asked several of us he trusts as loyal patriots to keep an eye on these agitators and report their activities and associations back to him. I have need of a woman to act in a clandestine operation designed to get me within the social circles of some of the local questionable citizens."

Watching his eyes she can see that he is sincere in his words, or so she believes. "How could I be of help?" she asks.

"You have the look, the mannerisms and speech of a sophisticated woman of the world. I and my colleagues are convinced that you would immediately draw their attention and be invited into their inner circles. As your 'husband' I would naturally be included."

"If I should agree and am seen through, then what?"

"We do not feel you would ever be in any danger," he lies, "I only want you involved when I am there to provide protection should it be necessary. In a few weeks you can disappear into your anonymity, no one the wiser."

"Mr. Palmer, I am a married woman and will do nothing to bring dishonor upon my husband."

"How could your helping your country bring dishonor on Richard or yourself?" he questions.

"How do you know his name?"

"You signed in at Mrs. Daubeny's as Mrs. Richard Jewell."

At this she begins to realize that she has been watched and followed. "I am uncomfortable with your intrigue and skulking about."

"The nature of the business I'm afraid. If it bothers you I apologize but you must understand that we must first ascertain the loyalties of anyone we bring into our confidence. We know your husband sells land on the New York frontier, that his and your fathers both served as volunteer militia scouts on the patriots' side during the Revolution, that your two uncles fought with the militia in Massachusetts and one was wounded."

"Under what name would we operate and wouldn't my having signed in as Mrs. Jewell be a problem?"

"Mrs. Daubeny is a loyal patriot and is working with us. Her records already reflect our union. The records of your and Mrs. Martin's stay have disappeared also. The cover story is that I was in Albany procuring cattle for the army and that you went on from there to Boston to visit relatives and that we planned to meet here. Our targets have estates out on Long Island and probably aren't aware of either you or me until we checked into Mrs. Daubeny's. She has assigned us adjoining rooms and your things have been moved so we can put on an act of husband and wife and you can retire to the safety of your own room."

"Much of what you say overwhelms me and I fear my lack of ability to pretend as you require," she laments.

"You only need to watch what you say that might give you and me, by extension, away. Moments when you are most relaxed can be the problem. Are you prepared to engage in the adventure of a lifetime?"

"Strange that you should put it that way. I left home to find a way to put my brother's death and that of others out of my mind and I told myself that I needed some sort of adventure to do that."

"Life on the frontier can be fraught with tragedy," he says knowingly, reaching up unconsciously and rubbing the scar on his cheek with a far away look in his eyes.

"I am willing to try as long as you understand that if I decide to quit, I can," she states.

"We will be attending certain local social events in an attempt to gain their confidence and will probably never be far from a crowd so you should be able to pull it off easily," he contends continuing, "When we get back to the boarding house we will eat, then when we go to the room another couple will join us briefly. They are acting as our backup and you probably won't see them again as tomorrow their disguises will change."

Rising as he does, she easily takes his arm and they stroll on that way appearing a quite normal couple taking an early evening walk. At Mrs. Daubeny's she greets them as 'the Palmers' and the ruse begins.

Supper out of the way, during which she has addressed him as John, they climb the stairs and he leads her into a room with a large parlor where a couple about her same age is waiting. Introducing them as Elizabeth, a pretty blonde with a nice shape and David, a well groomed, dark man with a scar on his right hand. Palmer says to the woman, "Show Bertha her room and see that she is comfortable while I and David plan tomorrow."

Exiting a door from the parlor the two women enter a spaciously appointed bedroom obviously decorated to make a woman feel comfortable. "Go ahead and unpack honey," the woman says, as Bertha catches a slight drawl in the voice.

"Where are you from?" she asks her companion.

"Caught the accent did you? South Carolina," comes the answer.

"Charleston?" Bertha asks.

"Yes."

"I'd like to visit there."

"Maybe when this is over, I can have ya'll down."

"Richard and I'd like that, Elizabeth," Bertha says.

"Please call me Liz honey, here, John wants you to hide this under your clothes whenever you are out. Just in case. I know he promised that you would not be in danger, better to be safe than sorry." She hands over a thin stiletto in a silk case obviously designed to be worn like a garter. "See I have one," raising her dress and petticoats to reveal a similar weapon attached high up her right thigh.

Bertha momentarily blushes, never having seen a woman so freely expose herself before, realizing that the woman's pantaloons were very short to show so much skin. "What else that he said should I be wary of?"

"Honey, John is very good at what he does and you should relax and not worry yourself."

"How long have you been doing this," Bertha asks.

"Can't discuss that, just know that we will be near if you need help. Now come on the men will be ready for us."

Bertha

The four of them then make plans to attend a concert at a theater that evening. Bertha is briefed on the appearance and background of the intended target of the night. She listens raptly and can feel the excitement rising in her bosom. This is going to truly be an adventure beyond what she had ever thought to find. Privately she prays that she can pull it off rehearsing over and over in her mind referring to Mr. Palmer as 'John' or 'dear' which seemed to come the hardest.

While she dresses and arranges her hair for the evening she keeps telling herself to relax and be herself. John has said she must not speak of being a teacher but rather present herself as an indulged childless, housewife, slightly bored with it all but obviously brightened by the sophisticated company. That he is an Army cattle buyer is something she tolerates but holds out for him to better himself. The ruse seems simple enough and she warms to her part the more she contemplates it.

The couple they intend to get the attention of owns a large estate out on Long Island and they often entertain persons known to be sympathetic to Great Britain. Most of them are relatives of British Loyalists that lost their estates at the end of the War for Independence. British agents are known to move among them stirring up animosity and a desire to return the landed gentry to power.

Mr. Palmer's group is to ascertain who makes up this cadre of disenchanted citizens and the identity of the British agents moving among them. President Jefferson has made a direct inquiry of Mr. Palmer to obtain the intelligence.

Guided to a box to the left of the stage and raised above it, Bertha soon spots their target across the theater in a larger box with several couples in attendance. The female is dressed in the latest fashion and much animated as she talks with her companions. Her husband, as well dressed, appears to be more reserved and spends most of his conversation on an equally outfitted gentleman to his right.

John leans to Bertha, "The assistant to the British Ambassador, that's his son and his wife directly behind him. We suspect him of a lot of the agitation in those quarters.

We hope to hear him make direct remarks that will implicate his treachery." The lights go down and the performance begins.

As preplanned when intermission began John guides Bertha near the party in question then he makes as to be needed elsewhere leaving her looking a bit abandon. The Ambassador's son ever aware of any beautiful female and always ready to offer assistance steps to her, bows and says, "Madame, I couldn't help but observe that your companion has abandon you, might I be of assistance getting you some refreshment?"

"Most gracious of you sir, but I would not want you to neglect your wife."

"She is deeply engrossed in conversation and will hardly miss me," he assures her.

"Very well, then. A gin would be fine, thank you."

In a couple of minutes he is back with two drinks in hand, "Madame, I must introduce myself, I am Edward Collingsworth and that is my loving wife, Harriet. We are here as guests of my father, the British Ambassador's assistant for trade, as are our other companions."

Accepting the proffered drink, Bertha replies, "Bertha, thank you sir. My husband, John Palmer, is in town on business and we decided to take in tonight's performance. It is so boring back home." She emphasizes 'boring' with a disdainful look and tone of voice. "I do so enjoy getting out among people that value the finer things of life."

"If it pleases you Mrs. Palmer, I will introduce you to our little group," he offers.

"You are much too gracious, sir."

"No, please meet them, they will be most pleased."

Taking her elbow he leads her to each of the gentlemen and women in the group. She is immediately drawn into a conversation on the quality of tonight's performance that is cut short when the second act is announced. As everyone heads toward their seats, John appears as if from nowhere and guides her back to the box. "How did it go?" he asks.

"Probably better than you thought," she relates, "I was introduced to everyone. Mr. Collingsworth was very gracious and attentive as you predicted."

"Fine, now we await a second opportunity," he says.

Just as the second act has ended an usher approaches John with a note which he accepts giving the usher a tip, the act of doing being seen across the theater. Unfolding the note he reads briefly then turning his eyes to the box opposite nods perceptibly to indicate acceptance. He then turns to Bertha, "Seems you gained us an invitation to Mr. Collingsworth's residence for dinner tomorrow."

Expecting things to move a little slower, John nevertheless is delighted to gain the inner circle so quickly. He cautions Bertha about topics of conversation and they agree to claim Cooperstown as home, giving her familiar things to discuss, he is confident the British don't have an agent that deep into the interior.

The next afternoon a ferry ride and short carriage jaunt out on Long Island takes them to the Collingsworth residence an estate he has rented while in the country with his father the assistant to the ambassador. The house being built after British troops had burned the original during the War for Independence is large and well appointed. The irony is not lost on Mr. Palmer, but he decides to remain silent about the estate's history.

The Collingsworths are genial hosts and make Bertha and John quite at home. It is not long into the conversation when John is aware that they are feeling them out about their loyalties. When it comes out that they call Cooperstown home Ed professes to have met the developer of the frontier town, Mr. William Cooper. Calling him a 'rough' gentleman he refers to Cooper's Federalist politics as leaning in the right direction.

John does not rise to the bait, claiming to not be very politically involved or having any dealings with the Judge, that his interest in the area was that it has a thriving cattle industry. Bertha disavows any interest in anyone's politics but does admit to having met Judge Cooper and found him to be quite gracious in his own way. Mr. Collingsworth takes this all in and remains in quiet contemplation. Harriet says, "I found Mr. Cooper to be somewhat of a pretender to gentility."

On the ride back to Mrs. Daubeny's, John allows that Collingsworth had been careful to not expose himself but had hinted that he is looking for like thinkers in the 'colonies' as he referred to the states either from habit or trying to elicit a response, John suspects the latter. It is plain that it would take other visits to 'smoke them out' as he said to Bertha. It did no harm that they had accepted another invitation for the weekend with others of the Collingsworth circle.

Back at the boardinghouse Bertha asks where David and Elizabeth are and he allows that they are never far away. This has Bertha wondering as no one she has seen has even suggested that they might be either of the couple. John just smiles at her obvious consternation, to be of the best help his agents don't need to be known that they are near. This particular team is especially adept at blending in, often fooling their boss.

Bertha's entry in her diary this night reflects the adventure and sense of danger she had felt conversing with the Collingsworths. She notes that she had not felt compelled to think about her brother's death or that of any others all throughout the day and evening. The next few days are to be spent with Elizabeth shopping and generally touring the sights of New York while getting indoctrinated for the upcoming weekend.

Wandering about the shops of New York City has given Bertha a chance to question Elizabeth about John and what she knows of his background. Knowing that he has largely remained silent about his past Elizabeth has to plead ignorance of most facts. The only thing she knows for sure is that he was in the Wyoming valley down in Pennsylvania as a child when Butler and Brandt and their hostiles had committed the massacre. That he had witnessed the killing of his parents and baby sister; receiving the wound to his cheek when he had tried to save his sister from being beat against the cabin wall. He had run off into the underbrush at night and survived only to come out the next morning and find all the bodies. Found the next day by militia coming to late to help, he was taken in and raised by one of them.

He is said to have avowed revenge and upon gaining manhood been several times to Canada searching for his family's killers. No one knows how many if any he has killed, but the story is that several former Loyalists and Seneca Indians have mysteriously turned up dead.

Bertha finds all this to be of great interest, giving her some insight into John Palmer's background. At the next briefing of the clandestine group, taking place after the weekend at the Collingsworths, it is decided that they have tapped the local 'loyalists' about all they should not wanting to give their true lives away. John says, "We have a similar setup going in Charleston that would not require Bertha's involvement." So it is decided that she should leave New York immediately so as not to be seen by any of those they had targeted. It being on toward mid-Fall and nearly time to reopen school she makes arrangements to catch a packet ship to Catskill from where she can return home via the 'turnpike' that runs across the Catskill Mountains to McDonalds Mills and on into the interior.

John swears her to secrecy, telling her not to tell any of this to anyone. He implores her to take him seriously, that her very safety could be in jeopardy should the British get wind of their work. Bertha assures him that she will remain silent and should he need her help later to answer the call.

Early the next morning she is at the wharf with her bags. Freed from the need to be ever cautious she is anxious to get back to Richard and the school. Strolling about the deck awaiting the fog to lift and the winds to pick up she suddenly finds her self face to face with a man whom she had seen at the Collingsworths.

"Why I do believe its Mrs. Palmer, whatever are you doing on a boat bound for Albany?" he asks.

Caught off guard she hesitates and then says, "John has gone to South Carolina to arrange for some Army cattle.

I found the prospect rather boring and decided to see family near Catskill."

"How delightful! This trip is looking up already and I thought that I too was saddled with a boring sojourn into the interior of this half civilized colony. Oh! Beg your pardon, state; I must discipline myself to the proper title. But it hasn't been all that long ago when I would have been right and it is so very possible that it could revert, hey Mrs. Palmer?"

"Why sir! How you do talk. I'm sure the gentleman jests?" she says casting her eyes around to see who might have over heard. At arms length away, a rather disheveled man with a beard talking with a striking red-headed woman carrying her things in a tied up blanket, catches Bertha's eyes and briefly, winks.

"Yes, yes, I jest," he smiles.

"Is that David and Liz?" she thinks too herself.

When she glances back they are gone. Able to report to John that Bertha will be fine and is safely out of the city and that she reacts well when pressed for an answer.

Chapter Seven
Finality

Hitting upon an idea, Ed Craft sets in motion a way to get near the Ward cabin during the day when Ann is teaching and William will be at work. About mid-day on Friday he says to his office help that he has forgotten papers at home and must go after them, vowing to return within an hour or so. Riding to the river ford he is soon headed up the mountain road past his home with no one in sight any where. "How lucky!" he thinks.

Jane has been watching the road for any body. She is delighted to see Ed Craft come over the rise and turn his horse up their lane. She steps out on the porch as he approaches. Dressed in a light cotton dress with no petticoats the west wind presses it back around her legs and her hair flairs out behind like a cape. Grinning broadly she waits for him to reach the hitching rail.

"W'y Mr. Craf' wha' ever brings you all th' way up 'ere?"

Touching his fingers to his hat brim he says, "I have often wanted to meet my neighbors and today seemed to present the perfect opportunity."

"To bad Will's at work jus' now," she smiles, 'ed wan' meet ya' too. Can I ge' ya' a drink?"

"Yes that is too bad, perhaps some other time?" he smiles back, "A drink of water would be fine."

Stepping back inside with a follow me wave of her arm Jane pours a fresh cup of water from a pitcher and hands it to him as he comes through the door. "This is nice," he says.

"Don' of'en 'ave company," she says, "an' Will won' be 'ome for hours." Plainly setting the opportunity for him.

"Don't you have children?" he asks, setting his cup on the table.

"'es at sc'ool th' 'yke 's ou' bac' play'n'."

"Nice," he smiles and reaches for her. A little too quickly, she is upon him pulling at his clothing.

"Slow down woman, let's enjoy the afternoon," he says, burying his face in her bosom. She has an unwashed mixed with cheap perfume smell about her. It only works to entice him.

"Wha' ever ya' say," she says, pressing her lithe figure against him. Catching the odor of tobacco on his hair she presses her lips to his ear, "Wha' ever ya' say."

Lifting her he moves to the bed in the corner. Leaning over to place her gently she hangs tight to his neck and draws him down atop her.

Later, quite pleased with himself, he dresses while saying, "I had a wonderful time, perhaps next time you can be a bit less in a hurry and we can extend our pleasure."

"Wha' ever ya' say," obviously pleased that he plans to return, "Ya' sure 'ave a wa' tha' ya' pleasure a woman!"

Striding out he hears the children exiting the school down the hill and realizes he will have to explain his early appearance at home; there is little chance he might get past unseen and return to the office. By the time that Ann arrives home he is settled on the porch with his pipe. Awhile latter William goes by climbing the mountain to home, he waves a greeting and Ed waves back thinking, "I hope she has rearranged the bed."

As these things go, Jane has been too pleased with her conquest to think about covering her tracks, so when William arrives home his eyes are drawn to the disheveled bed. Remembering that, like usual, Jane had straightened the bed while he ate breakfast, a thought that he had long tried to suppress surges up in his mind, "Would she be unfaithful? And who with?"

Jane sees him staring contemplatively at the messed bed, tries to cover up by saying, "I ha' a 'spell' 'his af'ern' and laid awhile wai'ing for i' 'o pass. Supper 'ill be ready soon."

"Now why would she need to give me an excuse for a messed up bed?" William thinks, taking his place at the table.

"Sam! Ya'll ge' in 'ere for supper, she calls to the boy playing in the yard, hoping to distract her husband.

"Saw fresh horse tracks coming up the lane," he states as if to no one.

"Dam'," crosses Jane's thoughts.

"Anybody come by?" William asks.

Cornered like a rat, Jane's mind races for an answer he will accept. "'hat lawyer Craf', he rode by to say hi. When I 'old 'im you 'ere at work he lef'."

"Funny, I saw him on his porch coming home and he only waved. No indication he wished to talk. Did he say why he came by?"

"Only 'o sa' hi," she says.

For the moment, William lets it lay there but his concerns have been alerted and he will be very watchful in the future.

Turning to Samuel he asks the boy how school was today. "The teacher keeps telling me to use correct words, when I talk like Maw does," the boy says.

"Miss uppity," his mother remarks through a mouthful.

Looking at Jane reprovingly, his father says, "You mind your teacher and you'll have a chance to better yourself and get somewhere in life."

"Yes, Pa. Can we go fishin' this Sunday?"

"We'll see, must watch the weather," William says, "Right now, eat."

Turning to Jane, William says, "Don't you dispute what Mrs. Martin or Mrs. Jewell teaches the boy! You hear me! He has to learn all he can to go on in life and become somebody! And you could try to learn some yourself, don't you know how ignorant you sound?"

"'eren' concerned in 'he bed!" she snaps back.

"Yes, and that goes only so far," he allows.

"Ya 'hink so?" she comes back thinking, "A lot he knows!"

Through all this Polly has toddled about the cabin chewing on a hunk of bread.

Having heard these exchanges before, Sam grabs up a piece of bread and flies out the door and down the hill to see if Nancy or Charles is about. It being meal time he knows he will have to wait for his friends to appear so he goes to where the creek passes their home and begins turning stones, looking for crawdads to use for fish bait.

By the time that Charles joins him he has his pockets full so the boys turn to other interests, Nancy. She has come bouncing down to the creek her red hair aflame in the late evening sun. While too young to understand, these two boys have been competing for her attention all summer. She has had a grand time being their center of attention.

Of the three of them, Nancy is by far the more adventurous, often leading the boys into forbidden or dangerous undertakings. Like the time out back of the school outhouse she had lifted her dress and pulled down her pantaloons to show them that she was different. Every since that adventurous, dangerous moment she had become the leader of the group, the boys seemingly unable to resist her ideas or even wanting to.

That single incident has been the soul move in the direction of sexuality; most of her ideas tend to involve challenging places or attempts. Like swimming the river or climbing Panther Mountain in search of the 'lost' Indian mine.

Harvesting about to begin, Ann had dismissed school today and the children now have all day to explore and examine their world of open fields, vast stretches of forests and river. The legends and stories of a hundred years of bringing civilization to this region paint an overlay of mystery and adventure that stimulates their young minds into many an adventurous idea. Charles Michael, now 11 is the biggest and strongest, then Samuel, at 10 a lean and wiry daredevil, easily stimulated by Nancy's ever daring escapades, as her fertile 9 year old mind constantly searches for new and challenging ways the boys can impress her. Joined, this summer, by Katherine, 7 the group has made most every tree and rock known to them from the Susquehanna to the high reaches of Panther Mountain.

With Bertha away, keeping an eye on this restless group has fallen largely upon Ann. Allowed, as a child, to roam freely, she tends to take the same approach relying heavily on Charles to keep them safe and back near home come meal time.

The Boyle sense of adventure has Charles willing to wander about experiencing the world even if Nancy largely directs each day's direction. Often her crazy ideas add mystery and daring to what would otherwise be a walk in the out of doors. He rather likes his role as the senior member of the group, but dislikes having to stop Nancy from goading Sam into some stupid or dangerous activity in order to impress her, which then he would have to copy to maintain his male ego.

This summer is proving to be quite a challenge for Charles because Nancy can now and does so quite freely; draw the younger Katherine into her schemes to stimulate the boys into daring do. While leggy enough to keep up with the older children, Katherine has yet to develop the coordination required to follow in every daring event. Charles finds himself spending time watching out for the smaller member of the group more than he would like. Picking her up and examining her scrapes and bruises. So far nothing bad enough that it has to be explained to Ann and Edward.

Taken fishing by his father on Saturdays, Sam is not part of the troop until later in the day. Charles is often asked to accompany them to the river. Some Saturdays Richard joins William and the boys, and they make a day of fishing, cooking on an open fire and telling the old stories over and over. The younger males love to hear of past exploits of their predecessors.

Seeing the Ward males accompanied by Richard and Charles headed down hill toward the river, Edward Craft does a stupid thing. With out a word to Ann, busy with her baking, he strolls off their porch and turns up hill toward the Ward cabin. Katherine and Nancy are playing along the creek, lost to their own interests.

A few hours later, the sound of a scream of terror disturbs the late morning quiet. The young girls stand looking up the hill from where the scream came. Down along the river the four males all turn their heads toward the sound.

"Could it be a panther?" Richard asks William.

"Don't think so, sounded more like a human, probably female," he replies, gathering up his gear. "We'd better investigate."

As the group of fishermen reaches a point, up the mountain road near the home of Ann and Edward, all seems quiet and serene. Continuing on toward the home of William they see a female form coming toward them with an ungainly gait.

Staggering into view, Ann with a knife clutched in her right hand is coming down the hill, seemingly unaware of the group coming up. Drawing close, the men can see that she is soaked in blood. Richard reaches for the knife and she lets him take it. William steps along side her and steadies her gently. "What has happened?" he asks.

"Everything's fine, now," she says.

"How did you get so bloody?" Richard asks, noting that she doesn't seem to be wounded. Turning toward her home he shouts, "Ed, your wife needs you!" There is no response.

"He's not there. Foolish girl tried to stop me. Didn't mean to hurt her," she replies. "Everything's fine."

"Take her into the house," Richard directs William, "I will go on up and see what has happened. Charles take the other children out by the creek, until I call for you."

"I want to see what's happened my self," William says.

"Charles can you take Mrs. Craft inside?" Richard asks, casting about for solutions.

"Yes," the traumatized boy says taking her arm.

"Sam you keep the girls by the creek while Charles stays with Ann, we will be back soon," Richard says.

They climb silently to where the lane turns to the Ward cabin. Almost to the front door, William surges forward and grasps Jane up off the porch floor. Naked, she is barely alive. Cut from her breasts to her pelvic bone her innards hang out around her grasping hands.

Richard can see that nothing can be done for the woman and leaves William holding her and rocking as he mumbles unintelligently. Stepping over the couple he continues into the cabin. In the corner bed naked, face down; lay Edward on sheets soaked with his own blood. His back shows several wounds where the butcher knife had been plunged to the hilt in an obvious fit of rage.

There being nothing that can help Edward, Richard turns to find Polly. His search takes him out to the sheds in back where he finds the child asleep on some straw oblivious to what has happened. Out front William rocks with his wife's body, she having expired a minute after being found. Screening her mother's body from Polly, Richard urges William to leave her lay and come with him. Slowly with a heavy heart William complies and takes his daughter's hand as they make their way down the lane. At the Martin's, little Polly between them Ann is no where to be seen. Once the men arrive she emerges from her bedroom, a fresh dress on and the blood rinsed from her hands neck and face. With a half grin she asks, "Can I get you some tea?" As if nothing had happened.

"No Ann, not for me," Richard answers, "I will leave you with William while I go for some help. I'll be taking Ed's horse."

"That's alright," she says, "He won't be needing it."

The two men look at each other in a silent awareness that she does not have it all together.

Turning to William she says, "I'm sorry, didn't mean to hurt your Jane but she came up from the bed screaming at me and I swung down at her. Only wanted to make him pay for his lies and treachery!"

Not sure what to say, William just nods and sets at the kitchen table as Richard directs Charles to take over with Polly and go get the other children and tells him that Sam or Polly are not to go to the cabin! He will ride to the settlement across the river and fetch help.

Ann busies herself getting out cold meat and bread for the children's mid day meal. The group of them soon tumbles in, full of inquiring looks and silent questions. Ann assures them that all is well and to get busy eating.

William sets watching it all in wonder. He knows he had suspected Jane was up to no good with someone but had never thought it would come to a head in this fashion. He knows he should be upset that this woman has killed his wife, but anger would not well up. All he can feel is the inevitability and senselessness of it all. He is fascinated that Ann can go on as if she had only excised a boil.

Samuel sets munching on his meat and bread not sure what to think about the turn of events. He had heard the scream and thought it his Maw and now Missus Martin speaks of harming her. Tempted to bolt for the cabin, only the calm presence of his father holds him.

A short time later Richard returns with five other men. They proceed on up the mountain, several with shovels over their shoulders, while he comes inside for William. Right behind the men a group of five or six women follow and they come into the house. Richard turns Ann and the children over to them and telling William to remain here while he follows the men on up the road. He hasn't gotten far when William catches up.

"My wife," is all he says.

Walking along Richard says, "I want you and the children to come stay with me at the house." In a way that it was more a command than an offer. William just nods.

Unceremoniously, the two bodies are wrapped in the very sheets they had romped on, carried out back of the sheds and buried in unmarked graves. No one says a word. William stands in the background and sheds not a tear.

Chapter Eight
Transitions

Having retrieved clothes and other possessions he knows Samuel and Polly will want, William stands with the other men when Richard exits the cabin. At first only a wisp of smoke follows him out the front door, but then smoke starts billowing through the roof covering and soon flames are consuming the roof. Promising to see to him and Sam's future, Richard had asked William's permission to burn the cabin. Glad to be rid of any reminder of his wife and their turbulent life together, William had said yes. The log walls burned for hours, making a glow on the mountain as twilight had settled in the valley. In the morning the smoke still rose with the morning fog. Full light finds a charred area of ground where the cabin and sheds once stood with two small spots of freshly disturbed earth to mark the passage.

William and the children have settled into a spare bedroom at the Jewell residence. Setting on the front porch in the early morning sun, William has tried to explain to Sam and Polly why their mother has gone away. It had been difficult explaining how making poor choices can ruin and often shorten a person's life. The boy seemed to accept and understand. Polly has no awareness of change except that her mother isn't around.

Samuel is upset that he will never see his mother again but he feels assured knowing that his father is there for him. In his mind, moving into the 'big house', as many call it, was a first step in going to the 'somewhere' that his Paw always extorts him to be working for.

A few days later the group of older children venture to the graves. Soon an argument breaks out among them, as to which is which. Sam walks away, not caring to know the answer. It is the last time he ever visits the site.

Richard and William return to their land work. Ann, reticent but concerned about the children's welfare, seems to go about her days as always, watching over all the children while the men work. Using that responsibility to mask her mental turbulence Ann pays particular attention to Polly. Determined that the child not come to harm and further upset William.

With Bertha away and not knowing how to address a letter to her, she holds her thoughts and feelings within. She busies her mind with thoughts of reopening the school with the coming Fall. The realization that Bertha would return soon, buoys her.

Richard, loath to admit it to him self, has begun to worry about Bertha. It has been over a month since he received her last letter and sent a reply the next day. He knows she promised to be back to open the winter school session and that was coming on soon. Already he has had a crew fill the school woodshed with firewood for the coming cold. Ann has been in the building preparing things.

After the tragic deaths the sheriff had come down from Cooperstown to look into the circumstances. He quickly came to the conclusion that the dead couple had brought it on themselves. Besides, Otsego County was not about to hang a woman for a crime of passion. After two days of poking around he rode off satisfied that justice had been done after Ann had admitted to intending to kill Ed and felt no remorse over killing the 'harlot'.

Then the day came when Bertha, after retrieving her horse in Cooperstown, rides up from the river ford and stops at Ann's to see her old friend. No one is at home here at mid-afternoon. Leaving the horse tied at the hitching rail Bertha walks the short distance to the school house.

Stepping to the doorway Bertha can see Ann puttering in the front of the classroom. "Hello, Ann," she says.

Startled, Ann whips around to see Bertha silhouetted by the light of the door. A few quick strides and she has enveloped Bertha in a great hug as the tears finally break loose. Not aware of what has happened, Bertha can only hold her friend until the tears and sobs lessen. Helping Ann to one of the long benches used by the students, she sets with her and takes her hands in hers, "Whatever has happened that has caused such a show of emotion?"

Bertha

"Oh, Bert, I have killed Ed and Jane Ward! It was terrible; I found them in bed together and just went wild!"

"No! When? How? I probably understand why."

"About a month ago, on a Saturday, William had taken Samuel fishing with Richard and Charles. I was in the kitchen baking and I saw Ed walk up the road and turn into their lane. I stood and fumed of a few minutes, and then I followed him intending to put a stop to whatever they were up to. When I walked in they didn't hear or see me, they were a rutting together on the bed. I wasn't even aware of having picked up my butcher knife as I left the kitchen. Suddenly I was plunging it in Ed's back with both hands. Jane began to screaming and came out from in under him and at me. I plunged the knife in her chest and pushed it to her crotch."

"How horrible for you!"

"I left them lying there and began walking home in a daze. Richard and William met me, nearly home still holding the knife. The sheriff came down and questioned me. He cleared me as being 'caught up in an act of passion'. I do not regret that either is dead, but I do have nightmares in which I am haunted by their mutilated bodies."

"Oh, dear Ann! My friend, what can I do to help?"

"Just that you are here will help. I have not been able to talk of this with anyone."

"Yes, yes! We will talk more but let's get you home where you can rest?" The two women walk to Ann's home leaning on each other, arm in arm.

Settled in Ann's kitchen with fresh cups of warm tea the two friends set and look at each other just glad to be together when Richard bursts in the door. He was coming home and saw Bertha's horse tied up out front.

As quickly as she can rise he has scooped her up in a hug. Lifting her off the floor and squeezing the air from her. When she can again feel the floor under her feet she gasps for breath around his kisses. She too feels great ardor being back with him but his lack of control has overwhelmed her and she can only think what would have happened if Ann wasn't there to calm his instincts. Smiling up at him she says, "I'm glad to see you to!"

Realizing that he has put on this display in a woman's presence causes him to regain control. "I apologize Ann," he manages rather sheep faced.

"No need to apologize, I am very glad you two have each other. As my friends you could never embarrass me by showing your love for each other. Now you two get on up to your home. I am much better now," she addresses to Bertha. "I will see you tomorrow. Then you can tell me all about what you've been doing."

On the ride up the mountain, Richard fills in around what Ann has already related. As they pass the pile of charred logs where the Ward cabin had stood, Bertha feels a sense of relief that that problem has been eliminated. How she is going to explain her whereabouts these past few months has not been set in her mind, yet.

"We have a new doctor in the settlement," says Richard, "Dr. Lindsay has built over near the mills."

"That is wonderful news!"

"William and I have been quite busy often selling smaller parcels surrounding the mills, it looks like a community is taking shape. We now call it McDonald's Mills. It now has two stores, one general and the other hardware, along with the two taverns or inns."

"Do I detect a note of pride in what you do?" Bertha asks.

"As well you may. I feel that your father's dreams are coming together. With each addition the area seems less a frontier and more a thriving community. Next I hope for a newspaper. For too long we have had to depend on the Cooperstown paper for our news. Some of us have been talking of the need for our own post office; again we have too long depended on the post from the Cooperstown office."

At that the couple have topped the rise and reached the front of their home. Dismounting they walk in hand in hand. Suddenly Bertha, feels a sense of relief at being in her own home.

It only takes a minute or two for them to reach the bedroom where they soon have shown each the love that they hold for the other. Lying sated they each know the other's heart with out words being spoken.

Slipping back into her dress sans the petticoats, Bertha proceeds to the kitchen and has water boiling for tea when Richard, dressed as casually in breeches with his shirt hanging out, joins her. Pouring two cups, Bertha indicates that they should set at the dining table. "I have much to tell you."

Taking in her natural beauty, Richard is deep into a feeling of joy at having her back. "Yes, tell me all," he remarks.

"At first I went to Albany then on to Worcester and took care of brother David's affairs, having all his assets transferred to Charles Michael. Mr. Brindle and I made a deal for him to purchase the farm and all that money went into Charles Michael's accounts. My little brother is quite rich in his own right."

"Not so little anymore, he grows into a handsome young man," Her husband responds, "Do get on with your story."

"After Worcester I went to Boston and made arrangements for additional supplies for the school."

"The shipment arrived several weeks ago and we expected you soon behind."

"Sorry to have disappointed you and sorry I didn't write more often of my whereabouts, but I got involved in something that I can't tell you much about. But I get ahead of myself," she pauses.

"You intrigue me," he says, wondering where her narration would lead now.

From here on she chooses her words carefully, feeling a need to be honest with him but well aware that she must protect Palmer's operations. "From Boston I decided to take a ship to New York City, wanting the experience of that form of travel. Again staying at Mrs. Daubeny's I took in a couple of performances and wandered among the publishers and book stores."

"Now what I am about to tell you must not ever be related to anyone, lives are at stake."

The solemn tone of her voice convinces him of her sincerity and he nods acceptance awaiting her words. He has never seen her this way noting her eyes darting about the room as if making sure no one was listening.

"I was approached to help obtain information on persons in this country who may be plotting with the British against our independence. That is all I can tell you, please don't ask more, as I have said, lives are at stake."

"Yours?" he asks, suddenly concerned for her safety. "What ever did you get into?"

"They did everything to hide my identity and assured me that once I returned home the people we dealt with would have no way to trace me. I believe they were sincere. That is all we must ever speak of this episode, please," she pleads.

"Alright, if you say so. But I still have my concerns," he says.

"Nothing more should come of it," she assures him, leaving out that the group could approach her again for help.

To distract his train of thought she moves around the table and stands next to him, taking his hand in hers, pressing it warmly. "I love you so very much and would not withhold anything from you that wasn't this important." Lifting his hand to her breast she intones, "Let's go back to bed?"

His response is to gently squeeze her and to rise sweeping her up in his arms all in one movement. They are soon back in the bed enjoying each other's strokes and kisses.

Sometime later they are awakened by a clatter of voices and footsteps downstairs, the children have returned from their afternoon adventures. The two lovers smile at each other and redress to get on with their lives. Bertha is looking forward to seeing each child and has a conversation in mind she intends to have with each. Richard, back in the euphoria he had experienced earlier, puts aside his concerns for now and just enjoys watching her cover her beautiful nakedness.

Arriving down in the kitchen, Bertha is swamped with hugs and questions each of which she tries to respond to while taking in the changes each child exhibits. Samuel and Polly have accompanied the others and stands back watching the proceedings. Seeing them there, Bertha reaches out to Sam and draws him into the circle around her. He returns her hug, glad to be included in the camaraderie. Bertha has always accepted him like her siblings and the boy has returned the attention with a boy's devotion bordering on a crush.

Having answered most every question put to her, she directs Charles and Nancy to go to Ann's and retrieve their clothing as she wants them back in their own rooms tonight. Turning to Samuel she says, "I understand that you, your sister and father are our guests," as she reaches to draw Polly nearer.

"Yes'm, my Maw got herself kilt and they burned our cabin," he states matter-of-factly.

"I am very sorry for your loss; you are welcome to stay here. Would you mind if I think of you as another brother?"

The boy throws his arms around her and holds her tight, his head buried beneath her bosom, and then tears start streaming. A woman has not shown him this much concern, ever. To his mother he had been more of an inconvenience than a loved extension of herself.

She lets him remain until the tears stop and then taking him by the shoulders looks him straight in the eye. "Sam you are a great child, one that I have enjoyed teaching and I want you to know that I am your friend. I want to talk with you further but right now run and help the others get their things." She uses her dress to dry his damp cheeks, "Everything's going to be alright, now you get along."

"Yes'm," he says and is out the door to do her bidding.

She says after him, "It's killed not kilt, Sam."

"Yes'm," he shouts back at her as he clears the door in his enthusiasm.

For a moment she stands watching him go, contemplating what has just happened. Having watched her brother with Bertha, Polly now throws her arms about Bertha's legs and looks up with a grave expression. "No need to be concerned child," she says, "You are a welcome addition to the family also." A smile of satisfaction spreads over her face as she bends and hugs the young girl; she turns to the chore of preparing the evening meal.

Next on her agenda is an in depth conversation with Ann. So next morning she walks down to her home and the two of them settle in on the porch for a long talk with a cup of tea. Polly is allowed to wander the house while the two women talk.

"I am so very sorry you're marriage to Ed Craft ended so tragically," Bertha begins, "I had bad feelings about him from the start, in your place I would probably have done the same."

"Killing him had not entered my mind, it just happened at the time. I would not have harmed Jane had she not come at me at that moment. I hate her for enticing Ed but I hate him more for being open to her."

"I think I know how you feel; I'm just sorry I didn't kick her out after the incident with Jonah Preston."

"No way could you have known that this would happen, besides you and Richard wanted things good to happen for William. Has he decided where to live yet?"

"At breakfast he indicated he'd like to build a frame home over nearer McDonald's Mills. Richard and he are going to look at possible sites today."

"He'll make some woman a good husband," Ann says, wistfully, "Too bad it was I that made him a widower."

"Why Ann, I do declare! You say the most daring things!"

"You encourage me! A woman has to take her life in hand and best not wait for some man to decide what's good for her if she wants any happiness," Ann states.

"You'll not get an argument here," Bertha smiles.

"Well I'll tell you right out that I like having a man in my bed and don't intend to let too much time pass without one. Losing my husband was not planned and I see no reason for being penalized for it."

"My you do speak boldly and I'll admit that I feel a whole lot better about sharing my bed with Richard than I did sleeping alone these past two months."

"Were you ever tempted?" Ann asks with a grin.

"The thought did cross my mind, but I was never in an intimate situation that might precipitate a chance. I was too busy with other things to think much about my needs."

"Do tell!" Ann encourages leaning forward to hear well.

"I went to Albany, then Worcester and on to Boston where I made arrangements for more books and supplies for the school. Then I took a ship to New York where I had opportunities to attend some great performances and meet some interesting people."

"I see a flicker of your eyes! Tell me who he was!"

"Unfortunately I can't tell you more. Lives are at stake. Please forgive me but I can not elaborate."

"I can not believe that you won't tell me more after I have opened my most secret thoughts!"

"Ann, my friend, I'd love to tell you all but I'm sworn to secrecy. I could not tell Richard even."

"I'm not too sure I accept that, but if you insist?"

"I do, I'm afraid. Let's talk about the school; I've got plans for the next session and new texts to work with. This morning I sent the children to spread the word on school reopening.

Looking into Bertha's eyes, Ann can see that it would be futile to persist and not wanting to harm the friendship allows the change of subject, "Something interesting I hope, we won't have any new students this winter and those we have are bored with spelling and arithmetic."

"If learning about our form of government can be made interesting then we should stimulate their minds. I was able to find a text that contains the Constitution and guides us through its articles and amendments. I'm excited about the possibilities. Of course we must continue the tiresome rituals that assure competence in reading, writing and arithmetic but we can use the new material to help out."

"Show me what you wish to work on and I'll get busy reading up."

"Tomorrow the box at Young's store will be brought to the school and we can get started. We should open for classes next Monday if you can be ready."

"I have some concern about parents sending their children to a teacher that has killed," Ann admits.

"If no one has come forward by Monday we will open school as usual. If no students show up then we'll deal with it, but I think that if there was a problem one of the parents would have approached Richard."

"I'll be waiting for you in the morning," Ann says.

"You seem quite unconcerned about events, I want you to know that if you need to talk I am always available," Bertha offers.

"I am trying to function as well as I can but underneath I am a cauldron of conflicting thoughts and concerns. You have no idea how glad I am that you are here. If I have need, I'll let you know," Ann responds.

"Anytime," Bertha says, rising and hugging her friend. As she is preparing to go the three children, Charles, Nancy and Samuel come up the road and she hails them to join the adults on the porch.

"How did it go?" she asks.

"Got all the way up to the Houghtaling place," Charles says.

"Any messages?" she inquires.

"Most said their children will be there, is all," he relates.

Turning to Ann she says, "See, all is well. Come children lets get something to eat." The four of them head up the road.

"Nancy do these boys take good care of you?" she asks.

Charles nearly chokes. "Bert, she leads us around on one scheme after another," he declares before Nancy can respond.

"Oh, is that right," she reacts.

Nancy just smiles up at Bertha, her curly red hair bouncing as they walk.

Looking at Sam for a reaction, he acknowledges Charles' statement with a nod and a grunt.

"Interesting," thinks Bertha, "A female with leadership tendencies."

Over the next several months, thru Christmas and on toward spring, life has a regularity about it that becomes predictable. The snows had come with bitter cold and the first hints of spring have melted it from the exposed areas and opened the waterways . The white tailed deer can be seen on the south facing slopes, late in the day, browsing the exposed clumps of grass. Overhead the red-tailed hawks continue their incessant circling in search of an errant mouse or squirrel.

The students in Berth's school have practiced their letters and numbers to infinitude and get anxious to break away for the springtime activities. The boys talk of trout in the streams and the girls of a multitude of things that lead toward the natural urges of renewal. Nancy has again on several occasions enticed some of the boys into unwise activities behind the school's outhouse. Her crude attempts at being the center of attention are mostly of the innocent type but they have led a couple of the older boys into egging her on. This one day she and the boys are late returning to the classroom so Ann has gone in search of them. Rounding the corner of the outhouse she is appalled to see Nancy being held by one of the boys while the other is engaged in kissing her.

Grabbing each of the boys by an arm, she marches the three of them into the classroom, where Bertha dismisses the class so as to help Ann. Each of the boys gives the same story when questioned, that Nancy had invited them behind the outhouse to engage in kissing. That she had done so before with other boys. That they are sorry that they had gotten rough and that they promise never to mistreat a girl again.

Sending the two boys on home after admonishing them to keep their hands off of any girl, Bertha and Ann set Nancy down for a girl to girl talk although she seems too young to be so interested in boys in any way other than exploratory. Aware that Nancy has exhibited the ability to lead boys into daring-do, Bertha looks for an approach that she can use to explain to the child the need for her to stop enticing male aggression without damaging her childhood relationships with them.

"Boys like to impress you don't they?"

"Yes'm."

"Don't the girls like to impress you?"

"No'm and they aren't much fun anyway."

"Nancy, I have to admit to you that Ann and I too like to have the men impress us. But I think our reasons are different than yours."

"We are aware that your mother died before you knew her," Ann adds, "I know it's been hard being raised among boys and no close female for you to relate to."

"Your mother would not want harm to befall you. If you don't learn other ways to relate to the boys you could have great harm happen to you. Boys don't always understand self control and they can bring disgrace to an unwary girl," Bertha says, "While you are too young to understand the implications, I ask you to believe me that a girl should not encourage boys to touch her in anyway."

"You and Mr. Jewell have fun kissing," Nancy states, matter-of-factly.

"Yes, and when you get older you will too, but at your age such activity is just not permitted."

"I would like it if you and I became great friends," Ann says.

"Katherine likes you and we would both love to have you come see us, often."

"I like Kathy," says Nancy, "We play together with the boys a lot."

"And that's what needs to change," Ann says, "I don't want harm to befall Katherine any more than to you. Come play with Katherine anytime and if you'd like to talk, I'd like to listen."

"Yes, make it a point to play with Katherine. If you must include the boys make sure that it's where we can see all of you," Bertha says.

Not sure that she fully understands what has been said, Nancy nonetheless wanting these women on her side, promises to spend more time with them and Katherine and less with the boys.

"I will have a talk with Charles and Sam tonight," Bertha says.

"And I with Katherine," states Ann.

"From now on I think one of us should be out with the children and monitor their actions," Bertha says.

"I'll make that my job," Ann states, "Time for me to get home."

"Any men coming around?" asks Bertha as they walk to the creek crossing.

"I'm afraid they are all concerned with my past," Ann says, I certainly am not offering anything until I know what they might have to offer. There are always some that think a widow needs them without their bringing much to the bed, so to speak. I ran one of them sorts off, last weekend. My needs are real but I turn to alternatives before making a dumb mistake."

Continuing up hill passed Ann's house, Bertha calls back, "We'll go shopping once school is out!"

"Not that kind, I hope!" She calls after Bertha, with a smile.

Proceeding on up the road holding Polly's small hand, Bertha asks Nancy what she likes as her favorite subject in school. The little red-hard says, "Reading, ma'm."

"Do you understand what you read?"

"Most times."

"If you need help with words or whatever I'm here for you."

"Usually Charles can help me, you always seem so busy."

"Never too busy to help you, you must promise me that you'll come to me about anything Nancy. I promised your father to raise you well and you must help me do that."

"Was my father a nice man?"

"One of the best, honey. He and I were great friends, I miss him."

Trudging on up the hill the child falls quiet then asks, "Did he ever kiss you?"

Somewhat taken aback by the question, Bertha stops walking and looks at the girl's face. "No, we had a different type of friendship; we could share experiences and thoughts without getting physical. Your father was a handsome man in his own way and your mother captured his every interest in girls. One day you will meet a boy that becomes totally interested in you and he will treat you with every respect due a young woman." They continue to walk, soon coming over the rise near home with the child absorbing what has been said and Bertha noting to her self that Nancy seems older than her nine years. She must make an effort to reach within the child's thinking. "Probably has to do with the early loss of her parents," she thinks.

Just a month before school is to close for spring planting time, Bertha introduces the older students to the U.S. Constitution by distributing copies to each of them. "During these final days this spring and into the start of classes next summer I want you each to read this through. Starting tomorrow we will begin discussion of the articles and amendments. I would like each of you to pick an article and be able to discuss how it may affect you life. Those of you older boys that return in the fall should be prepared for an in depth discussion of the whole constitution. So while your hands may be busy until then, use your mind to read and think about what you have read, also ask your parents what they think. You young ladies will have your in depth discussion during the summer session. A campaign is under way to pick a successor to President Jefferson and we will be working discussions of this into our studies during the next month."

Bertha

That evening, Bertha calls Charles Michael aside for a much delayed conversation. "Charles, you have done exceptionally well in school, in fact, you have exceeded what I can offer and it is time for you to think about going to the academy in Cooperstown or some place in New England where you can further your studies. What ever you might decide, finances are no problem. Besides the trust that Father setup for you, all that David had has become yours."

"You mean that I own most of the lands that Father owned?"

"Yes, while Richard and I have paid into your trust for this house and ten acres as well as purchasing the office building over near Brink's inn, the remainder belongs to you. I want you to know all this while you contemplate your future. This community is emerging from it's frontier status and will need professional men of all sorts to guide and lead it into the future, it is my hope that you will be one of those men. Father worked hard to help establish this outpost in the wilderness, now we owe it to his memory to help it grow."

"Bert, I understand that you feel a need to continue father's legacy but I think of other things. I am not sure yet what I want to do, except that I have no desire for more school beyond what you can provide."

"No need to make big decisions just yet. I only want you to spend some time thinking about your future."

"Can we talk again, later?" he asks.

"Certainly, Charles we can talk any time. Can I ask another question on another subject?"

"Sure."

"I know that you are the eldest of the group when you, Sam, Nancy and Katherine wander the area. And, that Nancy often suggests doing daring and sometimes dangerous things. I hope that we can rely on you to control the situation."

"I often have to stop her from urging Sam into some daring-do. I do not like telling the others what to do."

"Ann and I intend to limit having the girls wander far with you boys. We wish to eliminate any chance for harm coming to any of you. But I do expect you to help me should to need arise."

"I will do what I can, but Nancy has a mind of her own!"

"We understand, Charles, just use your good sense and everything should be fine. One more thing, if you see Nancy getting into any situations with other boys please get her away from them and come to me or Ann for help, if you need it."

"Yes'm."

That night in their room, Charles tells Sam that Bertha has asked that they do not include the girls in their wanderings. Sam has no comment and is content to know that he and Charles are free to wander at will. The two of them make plans to go fishing right after school and so set their fishing gear out to be carried with them to school.

It is on this excursion and with Bertha's comments on his mind that Charles sets himself on a path that will take him to the Pacific Ocean. Setting on a rock with Sam while their lines drag in the river's current, Charles asks, "You ever wonder what's on down this old river?"

Sam, never one to spend much time thinking about things, says, "No. What do you think is down there?"

"This summer let's explore down river a ways?" Charles suggests.

"My Dad don't want me going far," Sam says.

"We won't go so far we can't get back for supper," Charles assures him.

"I guess that would be alright."

Chapter Nine
Explorations

For several years now, the newspaper printed in Cooperstown, the *Otsego Herald* has been available at the local taverns brought in each week by post courier. Richard has long made it a habit to pick up a new issue and bring it home with him. Thus, the latest news, articles of interest and advertising have been a part of the Jewell household for sometime now.

Left lying about where the children can read it, they have been exposed to ideas and made aware of goings on that many of their contemporaries would never know or think of. Encouraged by the adults the boys find themselves reading tales of exploration and adventure on the western frontiers beyond the Mississippi. That the expansion west would provide a sense of adventure to Charles Michael, son of an earlier westward moving pioneer goes without saying. His enthusiasm has been transferred to his friend Sam and the two of them spend their days acting out the exploration of the west by nosing about the creeks, ravines and forest on Panther Mountain. Nearly every daylight hour, not spent in school or doing chores, is spent exploring unknown places, fending off attacks of wild hostiles or otherwise creating in their minds, the stories read in the *Otsego Herald*.

Now in 1808 the newspaper regularly carries stories of the exploration of the Louisiana Purchase by the Lewis and Clark expedition. The very idea that someone could travel from the East, westward for months and find themselves gazing upon another ocean opened the imagination to vast spaces and adventures beyond what a young boy could come up with on his own. Charles and Sam are lost to the idea of 'Manifest Destiny' without knowing what it meant or how it would mould their lives.

At the ages of 10 and 11 the boys are limited to make believe adventures but by participating in them they build the very skills they would need to survive the harsh tests of the West. Charles seems to understand this in an unconscious way while Sam, just enjoys the adventure of it all.

That summer the boys would ask Richard and William to teach them to handle the rifle and pistol. After a short consultation they agree to do it. Once accomplished each boy is given a small bore rifle that he can carry about and practice with, after the admonishment that nothing is to be killed except for eating purposes. Thereafter the Jewell household has a steady diet of wild game on the table.

As promised, Bertha turns the school work to an examination of the constitution. Each morning finds many of the older students anxious to discuss what has been said in their own homes about what the constitution provides for. It is the elders in each home that add perspective by relating how it was under King George of Great Britain.

Living lives that are mostly with no contact with any authorities the young people of the times can only think that the way things are is the way things will always be. As the daily discussions progress a general awareness that this way of life is unique and in need of the protection of the constitution settles in the minds of the students and their adult teachers. For as things progress both Ann and Bertha gain in their understanding how the present way of life can encourage people to new ideas and accomplishments.

For herself, Bertha has gained a new appreciation for what John Palmer had engaged her in. Reading of more incidences where the British Navy was pressing more American sailors into service, she can see how the two countries are headed for a confrontation. It is obvious to her that certain persons in this country must be sending the British Navy information on the sailing schedules of American merchant ships in order for them to know where to find them so readily. Reading of these happenings has her longing for her past role and thinking of her past companions. She remains silent and goes about her daily routine wondering if they will ever send for her.

Summer comes and with it the summer session in school. Still working with the constitution Bertha guides the discussion to the fact that it is written for all the people but by it's very language places all these powers and obligations on men with no mention of women. She wants the summer class, being mostly female, to talk about the implication. The general thinking of the students' runs, that through their father or eventual husband each woman receives her guarantees. It is thought that while this seems a fine concept, what about voting? If the elected representatives represented them all why aren't women allowed to vote?

It is here that things become somewhat heated. The young boys have gone home and reported that Bertha had said that the women should be able to vote. This being a presidential election year, this new right or obligation, depending on your bend of mind, was looked upon by most men folk as theirs, not to be bantered about by women.

A meeting of parents at the school is called for. Bertha finds herself having to defend her comments to a largely disagreeable group of men while the mothers sat by silent. She agrees, in the interest of the children to refrain from further discussion of this type with the children, while refusing to withdraw her contention that women should have the right to vote, same as men. The seed of disenchantment planted, the theory grows and joins with other voices that will bring about change, years from now.

Richard, up to now unaware of his wife's thinking, finds himself rethinking his position. Being male and qualified to vote he has never given thought to giving Bertha or any woman the same privilege. He can understand where most men think themselves best qualified to make these decisions, seeing as how they are most likely to have knowledge of the issues. He has never thought about the situation from that of an educated woman. He has to admit to himself that Bertha and probably Ann are as apt to make an informed choice as any man in the community.

At supper that very night Bertha puts it to him. "Do you think women should be able to vote?"

"To have you vote would not worry me but all women?" he says, hesitation in his voice.

"What would qualify any farmer over his wife, may I ask?" Bertha inquires, "I remind you that they do as much of the work as any man plus do the most toward raising the children."

"I do not oppose you in this but you cause us trouble by raising this question so openly."

"And why should it cause us trouble?"

"I fear that you could lose your teaching job and I know how much you love it."

"I'll not love it if I'm to not teach the truth!"

"Don't get all worked up, one day you may be proved right, but right now is too soon."

"May be right!?"

"Alright, alright so you are right now, but you're ahead of the times."

"I may be ahead of the times but I intend to move things along every chance I get," Bertha says defiantly, "Women are taking risk and aiding in the defense of the country and therefore earn the privilege to vote just as any man." Treading dangerously close to disclosing her activities last summer she thinks to shut up. Richard knowing that Bertha doesn't waste words is aware that she has let out a hint of that mysterious summer. They both let the conversation drift off.

Months pass and one day the cousin that had taken a farm up the Otego Creek valley rides into McDonald's Mills looking for Bertha and Richard. Directed to the land office by Aaron Brink he finds Richard and William going over some survey maps.

His reason for coming proves to be two fold. He has received word that his father, Uncle Charles, has died of consumption and he goes to attend the funeral. Richard immediately takes him by the school and then up to the mountain home where Bertha soon joins them and gets the bad news.

Arrangements are made for Ann to take over at school and Bertha packs to accompany her cousin to Worcester. The next morning they depart post haste.

With Uncle Charles buried the Boyles have a family meeting. His son, by now aware that the Otsego County farm is playing out, informs them all that he intends to move his family west, probably to Ohio or Illinois. There is plenty of prime land opening up out there and he feels a chance to better himself. He offers to take his mother, Mary with them. With her husband dead and all the children gone she sees little reason to remain. Soon one of Michael's sons is asking if he and his wife and children can go along. By evening time a whole group of Boyles are included in the plan to move west. Only Michael and his wife, saying that they are too old for such an adventure, are to remain in Worcester to oversee the Boyle holdings with plans to sell them off and forward the value to the appropriate family members.

The very next day they set about obtaining the wagons necessary to make the move. It is decided that Bertha and her cousin would go on ahead so he could get his family packed and the rest of the family would follow as soon as possible, joining up with him at the mouth of the Otego Creek. From there they will raft down to Maryland then up the Potomac River and go by land over to the Ohio River and on to their destination. In fact, retracing the route taken by their Uncle James as he had chased John Swift westward.

Stunned by the swiftness of the planning, Bertha promises them a place to camp until the whole group is assembled. Then she and her cousin make the return trip to McDonald's Mills.

After the return home, Richard is not surprised that the cousin wishes to sell out and move on. Many crop farmers in the area have been doing the same. More and more land is going to pasture for cattle and sheep. He makes arrangements to sell the farm and forward the money.

Planning to catch the spring flood waters down the Susquehanna, the group has to hurry to assemble the wagons, food and supplies as well as build the rafts. Richard helps out by assigning a crew with raft building experience.

At the Jewell table evenings the conversation is mostly about the impending move. Charles Michael and Sam are fascinated with the activity, planning and prospects. Both youths are big enough to be of use helping build the rafts. While all this goes on they are not required to attend school and between themselves begin talking of going along.

When Bertha's cousin arrives with his family in late February, to await the others, the boys manage to let him know that they would like to go along. Ever mindful of the need for strong backs the cousin gives some thought to taking them. One evening with Richard and William relaxing around the campfire near the mouth of the Otego Creek, he broaches the idea. The boys are delighted!

"Would Bertha be opposed to young Charles going alone? And how do you feel about Sam?" he asks William.

"I cannot speak for Bertha, what does Charles say?"

"I am ready to go!" the boy chimes in.

"If you do go, would you return?" Richard asks.

"Hadn't given that a thought", Charles admits.

Turning again to William, the cousin asks, "What about Sam?"

"Sam and I are kind of between homes and I would like to keep him near me. But, looking at Richard he continues, I just might be interested in going along myself if Bertha wouldn't mind raising Polly until I can send for her."

Understanding William's position Richard only nods his acceptance, "I will sorely miss you William and I think that Bertha would agree."

"The Houghtaling boy can do what I do and just as well."

"Yes but you would be giving up all the good will you have built up in the area."

"Sooner or later I will have to move on and this just might be the best time, even though it comes suddenly."

"We have room on the rafts for another wagon," allows the cousin, "Having another man along won't hurt."

Turning to Sam his father asks, "Are you ready to go even if Charles doesn't?"

Looking at his friend, Sam replies, "I go where you go Father." Charles smiles back, knowing how his friend loves his father.

"Well Charles I guess we had better have a talk with your sister," Richard says.

She, at first, resists the idea of her lone brother and only surviving sibling leaving her protective circle. "You don't need to go west to make your fortune," she points out, "You have a small fortune in the bank in Worcester, Massachusetts growing every day."

"I have no interest in making money. I want to see those mountains out there and gaze upon the Pacific Ocean."

"You could do that later, after you reach full manhood."

"The boy isn't so far away, now," Richard says in support, "Going with an experienced group would teach him so much."

"Thanks," Charles smiles at Richard.

As they are assembled on the front porch, Bertha turns away and gazes out over the valley and community that their father worked so hard to establish here. "It would have meant so much to Father to have you here to guide this community."

"Bert, Father is gone and I have to do as I see fit for me."

"Yes I see that," she ponders, but ..."

"Once I have seen the Pacific I will return," he promises.

"I can only let you go knowing that to be a promise and that William will look out for you."

Elated, the boy grabs her in a great hug, "Thank you Bert, I promise!"

"You must write often," she further stipulates.

"Whenever I can."

Within the week the family members from Worcester arrive. With the ice gone on the river the wagons are loaded on the rafts ready to be turned loose for the run to the Chesapeake Bay. They await several lumber rafts to pass through, and then one by one, the five rafts containing ten wagons with seven families aboard are untied and allowed to slip out into the current. In minutes the last one has disappeared around the bend in the river and passed the Otego Creek. Bertha and Richard remain long afterward watching where they went and thinking, each their own thoughts.

With Charles Michael and Sam out of the house it has become almost too quiet for Bertha. Used to the hustle and bustle of the four children, she has difficulty adjusting to just her, Richard and the young girls, who spends more and more of their time when not studying or doing chores, down the hill with Katherine and Ann. In this fashion the months fly by with an occasional missive from her brother reporting their progress. The last of which tells of them all settling in the new territory of Illinois just Northeast of St. Louis, Missouri. Seemingly without effort, two years have slipped by since the Boyle Family has moved West.

On the international scene relations with Great Britain have reached their worse. There is talk of war in Philadelphia, each issue of the *Otsego Herald* tells of it.

Late into 1811 plans are formulated to invade Canada. All along the New York border with Canada strangers are seen skulking about as both sides employ spies to report on each others activities. In Otsego County talk is of support for the Army but everyday activities center on work and getting on with life. Business is good as government agents move about the area purchasing food stuffs for the growing army and navy.

Just after commencing classes for the winter session, Bertha and Ann are interrupted by two men bursting into the classroom. Commanding the children to stay where they are the intruders move to the front of the room. Pushing Ann aside they have a large feed sack over Bertha almost before she can react.

In less than a minute one of them has her over his shoulder and out the door while his partner stands with drawn pistol facing the aghast Ann and dumbfounded students. Slowly backing out of the door he says, "Nobody follow or they get this!" Then he too is gone.

Remembering the brace of pistols they had put in place years ago against trouble Ann grabs one and tosses the other to the oldest student, "Come with me," she commands.

Outside she only sees the receding head of the second man heading down hill toward the river. Turning to the student she says, "Get your horse and go for Mr. Jewell and help. I will follow as best I can. Hurry! Give me that pistol!"

The youth runs to his horse and rides off toward the ford while Ann a pistol in each hand follows the receding head downhill. At one point the second man turns and seeing Ann takes a quick shot. The bullet goes wide of its mark. To let him know she isn't deterred and intent on rescuing her friend she pauses long enough to return fire. Her shot, given more time to be aimed clips him in the right shoulder as he pauses to reload.

Dropping his firearm and cursing her he turns and follows his partner to where he is struggling to get a reluctant Bertha into a boat. With the distances closing rapidly between Ann and the men they don't have a chance to both get aboard the boat when she arrives within easy shot of them. As they struggle to get her friend into the bottom of the boat, "Just you two stop what your doing!" she yells, pointing the remaining loaded pistol in their direction.

Having already been winged by her, the one man tries to crouch behind his helper. "Careful Alex," he whines, "She can shoot."

"Careful with that," Alex says, "Ain't no need of anyone getting hurt."

Facing Ann, with one foot holding Bertha down, he slowly squats to the boat seat and withdraws another pistol. As he raises it toward Ann, she fires. The pistol had laid months since having its prime renewed, there is no flash and her pistol does not fire.

"Well ain't this just great," Alex says, keeping the pistol pointed at Ann, "Shove us off John and hop in. We are going down river. Like I said Miss, Ain't no need of anyone getting hurt." He lowers his weapon and sets on the seat taking the oars in hand. The wounded man pushes the boat off and jumps in. Bertha can be heard making muffled sounds from in the bottom of the boat. Ann can only watch

Ron Baldwin

helplessly as the boat fades out of sight around a bend in the Susquehanna.

Chapter Ten
The Search

Riding as hard as he can Richard, followed by the youth, arrives where Ann stands looking down river. "She's gone," she says, breaking out in tears of frustration, "I couldn't stop them."

"How long ago."

"Probably gone ten minutes. Said they were going down river," she sobs.

He is tempted to spur his horse in pursuit but knows that he could never catch them with the dense forest slowing him. The only reasonable form of pursuit would be by boat. The nearest is up river several hundred yards and he can't follow with no weapons.

To pursue Bertha's abductors Richard first gathers his weapons, bullets and powder, and a pack of spare clothes and food. He has sent Ann to town to raise the alarm and bring him assistance which soon starts showing up as several riders arrive followed by others. Soon a small crowd of men has gathered in the yard.

Richard asks for a volunteer to ride to Cooperstown to alert the sheriff. Jonah Preston steps up. "I'll go, Bert is my friend!"

"Thanks Jonah!"

It is then decided that Richard and three others would take two boats in pursuit. The volunteers go for their weapons, packs and sundries. Within an hour of her abduction two boats push off to follow down river. In hopes that they can get ahead of the kidnappers, two riders take the trail to Huntersville, though it is felt a slim possibility with a hours head start on the abductors part. The riders, if necessary, would continue on as far as Wellsbridge and failing to get ahead, would wait there for the boats.

With all haste the boats are pushed down the river, passing the Otego Creek and continuing on. Eyes alert for anyone along the banks who might have seen the pair of abductors. As the hours pass and there is no sign of those pursued, Richard's heart begins to sink. He cannot think of why anyone would want to take Bertha. The only activity is an occasional animal startled while getting a drink and the ever present red-tailed hawks circling and diving for fish. The silence, except for the slap of oars on the water and the screeching of the hawks, has the effect of depressing the minds of the pursuers.

By the time they near the Huntersville area they are exhausted from pushing the boats as fast as they can row. It has now entered the mind of every man involved that this could be an impossible task trying to catch a boat capable of moving as fast as they can. As they approach two men tending a fishing weir, they are told that no boat has been seen but that a rider had passed a few minutes before spreading the alarm. It is agreed that the hunted boat could have passed earlier as these men had only been on the river an hour. Things begin to look grim and Richard is crestfallen and disappointed as the reality of the situation sets in. It is decided that one boat would continue on to the rendezvous point with the riders while the other would return by rowing and poling. Richard continues on.

Back up the valley, Bertha's abductors anticipating a quick pursuit have rowed to the Otego Creek and then up it about a mile where they have secreted three horses. Once obtaining them they transfer their burden to one, and tie her across the pack saddle. Careful to hide the boat where it would avoid detection for months, they then work their way up the Otego Creek valley avoiding the settlements until arriving where they have a wagon waiting near where the road to Laurens and beyond can be utilized. Placing two of the horses in harness the other is tied to the back of the wagon. Their luck holding, having not being seen so far, they place Bertha, still bound in the sack and now gagged against making any sudden noises, in the wagon and cover her with hay. When they meet a farmer bound for McDonald's Mills they appear to be just locals about their business. Pleasantries are exchanged and all continue on their way.

For her part, Bertha has decided that resistance is futile and only results in rough handling. She had decided that if they meant her harm they could have killed her at most any time. Husbanding her strength she awaits an opportunity to escape.

Reaching Wellsbridge where the riders wait, Richard realizes that this could become a long search. What he wants to know is, "Why Bertha? Is this somehow tied to that mysterious summer trip? Where can I find information? Where can I find Bertha? What to do next?" No answers being readily available he determines that they should all return home and rethink the situation. The riders exchange the horses for the boat so Richard can get back home faster. It takes until the next evening for the two boat crews to return to the community.

Riding back up the trail toward McDonald's Mills, Richard and his companion have to ford the Otego Creek where they pause and let the horses drink. Setting there he wonders, "Is it possible that they came this way? And how would he ever find out?"

Back at the house he sets on the porch overlooking the valley and passing possibilities through his head when the sheriff and a deputy come up the lane. Inviting them to dismount and set with him it only takes a few minutes to apprise the sheriff of what he knows. The three of them set gazing out at the vastness of country before them and are at a loss as to where to start looking. The sheriff says he will have his deputies out talking to the settlers and inquiring has anyone seen any strangers moving about. He doubts that they could get far without being seen by someone. Perhaps his deputies could find a lead. He is mainly concerned that the kidnappers have successfully slipped down the Susquehanna without detection at least as far as Wellsbridge, much beyond there and they would be out of his jurisdiction. While Richard agrees that that might be possible, in his mind he has been thinking that they may have fled up the Otego Creek and shares this with the sheriff. It being a very possible idea, he sends the deputy with him to immediately start checking the settlements up that valley. With nearly a day's head start it is understood that the trail is getting cold.

Looking at all possibilities, Richard tells the sheriff about Bertha's trip in 1808 and the mystery surrounding it. The sheriff thinks that with war talk abounding and his getting warnings and bulletins to be on the outlook for possible spies, that her past activities may in some way be tied to her abduction. No one can think how that might be.

Up along the Otego Creek valley, well removed from the McDonald's Mills area, the kidnappers have stopped for the night at a log cabin on a recently abandon farm and begun the process of extracting the information they have been sent to obtain. With Bertha securely tied to a post in the cabin they have been taking turns questioning her. Last night and through the early morning hours they have continued.

At first, letting her know that they know all about her by relating her family's history and her recent movements, they attempt to get her to reveal her participation in the spying on British citizens in the country and their connections with certain Americans. She remains silent.

Listening to them relate all the information about her background, she is aware that they have dug deeply into her past. That she may have participated in spying on the persons in question seems to be more of a conjecture than known fact to them. She vows to remain silent.

After a few hours of this, it is evident that the one Ann had winged is becoming nervous about remaining so close to where they snatched her. He steps close to her and says, "Come now Mrs. Jewell we know of your activities and we know that you were part of a group that spies upon certain persons. What we need prior to letting you go is confirmation of your activities and the names of your accomplices. All you need do is give us what we ask then we'll let you go none the worse for wear and we'll be off to Canada."

Bertha looks him in the eyes and says nothing. Being tired of standing tied to this post with only fitful sleep and thirsty she asks for a drink by saying, "Water."

The wounded John tells the burly Alex to go to the spring for fresh water. Getting real close to her face John speaks softly, "We ain't leaving without the information. It's up to you how we get it from you. Up to now I have tried to treat you respectfully, but we can get rough if necessary. Do you get my drift?" As he runs his fingers down the front of her dress and his eyes lock onto the surge of her bosom.

Still refusing to speak she nods her understanding. Her eyes show defiance as she feels at the bonds holding her hands behind the post. She seems to be securely bound.

Alex returns with water and holds a cup so she can sip a few drops. "Thank you," she says, her eyes softening to him. He has a moment of connection with her, having already decided that he likes this feisty and, as his hands had found out, well built beauty.

He smiles briefly in reply, "Did she say anything?"

"No," says John, "But she now understands the gravity of her situation. We'll have a bite to eat then see if she is ready to talk. Start a fire and we'll eat a hot meal."

Alex sets about building a fire in the fireplace while his partner gets out the fixings for a meal. Soon the cabin fills with the smell of biscuits baking and bacon sizzling.

Out on the road the sheriff's deputy has learned that a wagon with two men aboard was seen going through Laurens late the past afternoon and that the storekeeper, who had seen them did not recognize the riders. Besides it was unusual to have two men in a wagon and only one horse tied on back.

With this information the deputy continues riding North toward Hartwick his instincts telling him he is on the trail of Bertha's kidnappers. "What to do? Should he return with word or send someone back? Should he deputize a few locals to help in case he comes upon them?" These thoughts racing through his head he suddenly is aware of the smell of bacon cooking.

Reining in his horse he looks about to ascertain the wind direction. Learning that it comes from the west where a log cabin sets back against some tall white pines on the high ground across the creek, he sets a moment then can see a wisp of smoke coming from the chimney. Such a brazen lack of security convinces him that it is only a settler's wife cooking supper for her family. Because the cabin commands a good view of the road he thinks to check and see if anyone has seen the wagon go by.

The deputy heads his horse toward the lane where it crosses the creek and goes up to the cabin noting as he does that, the most recent wagon tracks lead toward the cabin. At this time, Alex has steps to the door and sees the rider coming their way. "Company coming up the lane," he barks.

"Get in the yard and see what he wants," directs John, "I will keep our guest quiet," and he takes a handy rag and stuffs it in Bertha's mouth. She gags on it and John gives her a warning look.

Pulling the door closed behind him, Alex waits for the rider to approach the cabin. The late afternoon sun catches the deputy's badge and warns the kidnapper. "It's the law," he growls under his breath, hoping that John has heard him through the closed door.

In the cabin, her captor has stepped close. Upon hearing his partner's growled warning he has drawn a knife which he holds against her throat saying low, "Not even a groan or it'll be your last." Bertha stiffens feeling the sharp blade against her skin.

Out in the yard Alex hails the deputy, "What brings you to these parts?"

"There has been a kidnapping down at McDonald's Mills. Any chance you saw a wagon with two men headed north on the road yonder?"

Alex is not happy that their trail has been crossed so quickly but the rifle carried by the deputy points casually in his direction and keeps him from making a move to the pistol jammed in his own belt. Attempting to keep the deputy relaxed and off his guard he says, "Why yes, an hour or so ago I was splitting firewood and saw a wagon going up toward Hartwick with two men as you describe. Too far away to make out whom they might be. A kidnapping you say, who?"

"The wife of the land agent there."

"What ever would anyone want with her?"

"We don't know just yet, but must be something important. This is the first kidnapping, not by Indians, in all the years I've been a deputy. That's mighty good smelling bacon."

The Missus and kids have gone to visit family over toward Morris," Alex lies, "And I threw a few strips for myself on the fire," Hoping to dissuade the deputy from staying he purposely fails to invite him to share.

"Well I suppose that I must be going, don't want to get any further behind their trail. When did you say the missus went to Morris?"

"Just this morning."

"Uh-huh," the deputy responds knowing that no wagon or horses had been down this lane since yesterday. He reins his horse toward the lane, "See you again someday." Alex watches him reach the road and turn north before reentering the cabin.

On Panther Mountain, Richard is going crazy with not knowing which way to turn or why this has happened. The sheriff has remained at the Jewell home in hopes of any lead he can react to. Early on the second day he has sent instructions to his deputies to fan out to the west and dispatches via the post couriers to all authorities down river and up to Johnstown who will relay it on up the Mohawk valley. He tells Richard that all they can do now is wait. Waiting with Bertha missing is something that, Richard cannot do well. He paces about the house and out on to the porch at every noise, thinking it might be someone with word. Not content to continue doing that Richard, thinking about what could have happened that mysterious summer that could have precipitated this, remembers that Bertha spends a lot of time writing in her diary. Retrieving it he begins leafing through the pages looking for dates that coincide with that summer. Finding the corresponding pages he reads of John Palmer and his organization of spies. It doesn't take long to realize that current events could well be tied to this activity.

The sheriff by now is expecting the deputy he dispatched up the Otego Creek valley to report in either himself or by sending word via a rider. Richard brings him that part of Bertha's diary that helps to explain the turn of events. Soon thereafter, a rider from up near Laurens arrives with word from the deputy. With the day wearing on the Sheriff, Richard and several quickly deputized citizens ride out for the village up along the Otego Creek.

In the cabin the two kidnappers are arguing over what to do next. John keeps looking menacingly toward Bertha and insisting they force her to talk now so they can leave the area, not convinced that the deputy was put off the trail. Alex, on the other hand, does not want to be a part of torturing her to get her to talk and argues to put her back in the wagon and flee northward.

The deputy, going on his instincts, has ridden north just long enough to get completely out of sight then circled back south toward Laurens in hope of sending someone to alert the sheriff while he keeps an eye on the cabin. He is convinced that the man in the yard lied to him and for what reason?

Bertha for her part has a plan of her own. She has not been allowed out of the cabin to use the outhouse since early morning. Now as twilight is settling on the valley she sets her plan in motion. "If you really intend to treat me properly it would be nice if I could use the outhouse."

Her sudden words interrupt the arguing and the kidnappers realize that she has gone all day without relief. Alex steps behind her and releases her bonds. John cracks, "You get two minutes then we come in! Take her out and keep a hold of her until she is in the door."

Holding her gently by one arm Alex walks with her to the outhouse. "Be quick about it," he warns as she draws the door closed behind her.

She does as she has to so that he can hear her water in the quiet surrounding them. Then rearranging her clothing she sets down on the seat and draws her legs up with her feet just inches from the back of the door. She remains this way until Alex, getting impatient with her, steps up to pull the door open. Upon seeing the movement Bertha slams both feet against the door, knocking her abductor backwards onto his back causing him to hit his head violently on the ground. He is stunned.

As quickly, she has gained her feet and leaped over his prone body and toward the cover of darkness under the pines behind the cabin. Meaning to gain as much distance as possible before the stunned man can raise the alarm she flees headlong through the grove of towering trees.

John has completed cooking the meal and placing the food on the table looks to see if they are returning. Not seeing their approach he steps out into the twilight to check. With the outhouse set back of the cabin he must first round the end before he sees his partner trying to gain his feet and no sight of Bertha. He rushes forth just as Alex begins to partially regain his senses. "Where is she?!" he shouts the question, futilely.

Alex, barely able to stand, is unable to provide an answer. He stands rubbing his head and becoming aware that it is his lax handling of the prisoner that has allowed her escape. "Sorry John, she surprised me," he pleads.

"Get down the lane and head off an escape that way!" John commands, "I'm going through the pines!"

The two men separate to hunt for the escapee, while she, attempting to put as much distance as possible between her and the kidnappers, crashes out through the brush along the creek and falls into the water. The splash in the night alerts two men. John heads toward the sound and the deputy, who had been working his way to a place where he can keep an eye on the cabin and its inhabitants, turns that way.

Proceeding quietly the deputy approaches Bertha who is trying to wring as much water as possible from her clothes, just as John grabs her from behind. Struggling to remain free she kicks out and places painful hits on his shins and he releases his hold. She spins around and slaps him up side his face causing him to stagger. As he regains his feet he stands staring past her at the rifle muzzle pointed his way.

"Keep back or I'll shoot!" the deputy warns.

On hearing the voice, Bertha again spins around to see her rescuer a few feet away. "Step aside Miss so I have a clear shot," he says.

"There is another one," she warns.

"I know, I met him earlier," the deputy says, "We should be going before he arrives."

At that moment a pistol barks in the night close by and the deputy suddenly hit from behind, discharges his rifle the bullet slamming into John's chest. Bertha's kidnapper, eyes wide at the suddenness of the blow, falls backward into the creek dead, his blood swirling in the water.

The shot from behind, hits the deputy in the shoulder and while causing him to squeeze the trigger, does not cause him to drop the rifle. Retaining hold, he too staggers a couple of steps and then turns toward his assailant, who is still groggy from hitting his head on the ground and can't quite understand the turn of events in the dark and why he has not killed the deputy. The two injured men face each other each unwilling to assail the other.

Bertha takes a moment to sort things out herself then steps to the deputy and draws his knife. Pointing it at Alex and threatening to cut him she suggests that he drop the empty pistol. He does, still confused over who has the upper hand. The deputy performs a one armed reloading of his rifle and the situation becomes seemingly stabilized.

A few miles away, just above the village of Laurens the sheriff is arguing for the posse to wait for first light to approach the area indicated in the message from his deputy. Richard is anxious to press ahead even though he does not know the exact site of the log cabin. The sheriff has prevailed upon the others when two shots are heard from up the valley a mile or so. One is definitely a rifle and the other sounds more like a pistol.

With Alex leading the way, Bertha half supporting the wounded deputy, follows behind, the rifle now in her hands. They make their way back up to the cabin and as they approach it her surviving kidnapper, his head cleared up, makes an attempt to get away.

Supporting the weakened deputy keeps Bertha from being able to react to Alex's moves. Quickly he has wrested the gun from her hands. Without her support the deputy has fallen to the ground and lays there unable to assist her.

In a few moments the abductor has again gained the upper hand. Keeping the gun on Bertha, Alex has forced her to help the deputy into the cabin, to put wood on the dying fire and to light a lantern for light. He now has her tied to the post again and returns to the interrogation. Propping the rifle against the wall he steps in front of her, the lantern light plays off his grim countenance. Slapping her hard across the face he intends that she understand that he has no more patience and intends to extract the information they were sent to get. She stares at him defiantly. "I will not break my word. You will learn nothing from me!"

"I will get the name I seek or you and this deputy will die by daybreak. I don't have time to be nice and will be leaving in the morning. If I have the information I seek I will leave you both alive, if not ...," his threat tails off.

Stepping to the deputy he pokes at his wounded shoulder with his foot until the man cries out. "Stop this barbarism!" Bertha shouts, "He has nothing to do with our situation."

Another flat handed slap across her face causes her to gasp and blood to run from the corner of her mouth, but she remains silent. From where he lays crumbled by the door the deputy says, "Tell him what he wants to know I believe he will kill us otherwise."

"Listen to the law, he knows how these things are done," Alex states.

"I cannot tell him anything, more lives than just ours are at stake," she testifies.

"Perhaps you will talk if my knife asks," the interrogator cracks, waving it before her face. Her look of defiance continues.

At that point the front door flies open, Alex dives for the rifle and simultaneous gun blasts rip through the cabin. The concussion causes every one there to be temporarily disoriented.

In the next instant Richard has cut Bertha's bonds and swept her into his arms. Their joy is overwhelming. The sheriff is glad to see that his deputy is alive and will survive and that Alex has joined John.

Having worked their way silently up the road the posse had seen the light and heard the deputy cry out in pain, which had turned them to the right lane and soon thereafter surrounded the cabin. When he had heard Alex threaten Bertha with the knife, Richard had had enough and burst in the door, followed closely by the sheriff who had dispatched Alex as he grabbed the rifle.

Untying Bertha, Richard is elated to see that she is unhurt. Seeing Richard burst in the door has given Bertha an overwhelming sense of relief. With the sheriff and his men gathering up the bodies, the relieved couple head for their home.

The original dispatches of the sheriff have reached eyes in Johnstown that have quickly relayed word of the kidnapping to John Palmer. As things are winding down at the log cabin Mr. Palmer and his right-hand man David, are riding hard down the trail to McDonald's Mills.

Bertha

Chapter Eleven
Preparations

With early light showing in the East, Richard and Bertha arrive at their mountain home. A few hours later the secretive John Palmer and David ride into McDonald's Mills and inquire of the Jewell home at Brink's inn. Both of them being strangers and offering no credentials, several local men surround them and demand to know their interest in the Jewells.

Assuring them that they are there to help rescue Bertha, many of the men say that they will accompany them to the Jewell home, just to be sure they are welcome there. With Richard and Bertha going straight to the house, word has not reached into the village that she is safe.

Having gotten some rest the Jewells are relaxing with a cup of tea on the front porch when a group of their neighbors ride up accompanying the strangers. Recognizing John and David, Bertha doesn't know how to greet them.

Palmer eases her mind by introducing himself to Richard, "Mr. Jewell, I am John Palmer and this is my associate David. We have come to assist in your wife's rescue but I see that has been accomplished with great results. I am anxious to learn the details. Can we discuss them in private?"

Looking at Bertha for guidance, Richard sees that she fully accepts what this stranger says so he thanks his neighbors for their concerns and assures them that these two are welcome. Turning to the men he indicates that they should enter the house. Everyone gets comfortable in the parlor then Richard begins telling how they had rescued his wife.

Palmer listens politely but he is more interested in who the perpetrators were and what exchanges took place between them and Bertha. Once Richard had related how he and the sheriff had determined the direction the kidnappers had taken, John says, "As usual in these cases some good luck turned your way, it seems obvious that they wanted information more than actually wanting Bertha. They must have thought that getting it from her would be the easiest source they could find. Obviously they were wrong. Now if you don't mind I have several questions for your wife then I will tell you all I can about what and why this has happened."

Turning to Bertha he begins, "Do you think you ever saw either of those men before?"

"Not that comes to mind, they seemed total strangers to me."

"Intentional, should things go awry; their commanders don't want any chance that the operation could point back to them. And they would not have any compunction against grabbing a woman they do not know. Unfortunately, seeing as how this attempt fell apart there is probably a good chance that they will try again. By interrogating her here in the interior of New York I'm sure they attempt to hide any trail into Canada. Otherwise they would have gone directly there before questioning her. Once word gets back that both kidnappers were killed and not questioned, another team will be dispatched. Now Mrs. Jewell, try to remember every word each of them said to you or each other. The slightest little comment could be of use to us."

Taking a deep breath she begins to relate all that she can remember start to finish. When she tells of them calling each other, John and Alex, Palmer and David exchange knowing glances.

"Amateurs for sure," David says.

Continuing to relate the conversations up until the time that Richard broke the door down, Palmer says, "You've done great! What you remember will help us a lot as we plan to thwart any further attempts to get to you."

"I don't like the idea that more thugs could be after my wife," Richard states.

David speaks up, "Now that we know that they have targeted Bertha as their easiest source of information, there are actions and preparations we can make that will most likely protect her from further harm. Once I send a message back to Johnstown, Elizabeth will join us and be your wife's constant companion." At this bit of information, Bertha smiles having great confidence in her abilities.

"Perhaps this would be a good time to tell Richard what this is all about?" Palmer says to Bertha hoping that she has held to her silence about his operations.

Getting a nod and an, "I've said nothing," from her, he starts.

"Because of the troubles with Great Britain President Jefferson asked me to set up an operation to monitor the activities of certain persons in this country. President Madison has asked me to continue my work. A few years ago your wife happened to be in a position to aid us in our work which she did, admirably I might add. I have operatives at work in many communities gathering intelligence on persons working against this country. Of course, the British would like to identify me and my agents. We believe that so far we are hidden to them. Your wife's silence under great duress has helped to keep us undetected. You should be proud of her strength and resolve in the face of grave danger. Of course, you understand that nothing of this can be told to anyone," John relates.

"We operate as cattle buyers for the Army," David says, "We would like to have that as part of why we are here, that we have met before when you were in Albany and we came to help out when we heard that Bertha had been abducted."

"That story should hold up, we have many cattle and sheep farms hereabouts," Richard says.

"Yes, we know that," Palmer says, "I apologize for putting your wife in jeopardy but it was felt that by living in the interior she was safe from detection. Obviously, a mistake, one which I hope to rectify, directly."

"John, when I left New York that day I ran into a gentleman whom I had met at the Collingsworths," Bertha states.

Cringing to himself, Palmer isn't happy that the Collingsworth name has been said but holds his council until later. He makes a note to speak with Bertha, that while

Richard now knows of the operation, names and information gained can never be reveled.

"Just how do you propose to keep Bertha safe? Do I have to take her from here?" Richard asks the concern in his voice obvious.

"It would be best for you to remain here, in this limited environment we can control circumstances better and give us a chance to spot strangers about. Do you have an office in the village?"

"Yes."

"Then it would be best for you to return to your routine and we will insert our team as best fits that. I assure you that someone will be close to your wife from now on. Didn't some of the Boyle family move west recently?" Getting a nod from Bertha, David continues, "I will stay as a distant cousin passing through, for a few days, until Elizabeth and the rest of the team gets into place. A few new faces will appear, seemingly unrelated in any way to each other. Just go about your daily activities. Should another attempt be made to snatch Bertha, we will be in place to thwart them."

"And if you are unsuccessful?" Richard throws out.

"Let's remain positive for now. As things develop the plan may have to be adjusted, but you should know we have done this before," says Palmer.

"You won't mind if I keep myself armed?"

"By all means, it would be a natural reaction to what has happened," allows David, "Now where do you put up traveling relatives?"

"I'll be going back to Johnstown, but will be kept informed regularly by my people. I want to thank you Bertha, for your loyalty in the face of danger. We will work hard to earn it," concludes Palmer. He leaves and rides off down the hill.

David is shown to a spare bedroom. After settling in he takes a long walk around the house and buildings familiarizing himself with the settlement.

That evening as they set for supper, Richard asks David, "What is your assessment of our situation?"

Bertha

"This is an excellent site to defend if necessary, but of course, I don't expect it to come to that. John's organization has been under attack on many fronts, mostly in highly populated areas. We have been able to fend off every attempt to take any of his operatives, Bertha being the exception. That they made a move here we feel shows a sense of desperation at their lack of success elsewhere. The situation has reached a point that this country is about to strike back, but of course I can not elaborate except to tell you that once hostilities break out the early part of John's operations, which Bertha got caught up in, loses it's importance. If the British are on to our plans to strike back then they probably will lose interest in your wife. It is John's hope that they continue to operate against his organization and by doing so are blind to what is planned."

"Otherwise you dangle my wife as a distraction?"

"I would not look at it that way. We are doing everything we can to protect her from harm. If they expose any major agents in an attempt to reach her again we will be in position to turn the situation to our advantage and capture them."

"How do you intend to accomplish this?"

"I can't discuss our plans much but I can tell you that we are moving several agents into the area posing in various positions as well as Elizabeth to be Bertha's companion. Her cover story is that she is a cousin come to visit. When she arrives I will leave but remain in the region. Believe me, the chances that any agents get past us and near Bertha and Liz are very slim."

"I would guess that we will have to take your word for that until something happens. I hope that you don't mind that I go about my activities armed. We live our lives here in peace and only feel threatened by an occasional animal, so carrying firearms has fallen out of favor. I'm sure my fellow citizens will notice that I go armed."

"With what has happened they will probably understand."

"Bert, you haven't said a word," David points out.

"I have every confidence in you and Liz but I want Richard comfortable with the situation."

"Liz should be here tomorrow, and then we'll get ready. If they come again I doubt it will be before long. It's getting colder and soon snow will make tracking easy. In our work stealth and the lack of any trace is essential."

The very next day, two clients of Richard's checks into Brink's inn and Elizabeth rides up to the Jewell home.

Bertha and Ann are conducting classes at school so the agent uses the time to coordinate with David. So when school is out and Bertha arrives home, Liz is awaiting her and David is gone. Glad to make her acquaintance again, Bertha greets the young woman with a hug and welcomes her to her home.

"Have you found a room yet?"

"I moved into the one David was using."

"That's fine; you see we have water just out the back door?"

"Took the liberty to inspect all the buildings and grounds. You have a nice and unique place here."

"We like it. My father built here first but that burnt and when Richard and I rebuilt we tried to improve on a few things. Glad you like it, but wish your visit could be under better circumstances."

"Lets make the best of it and you can continue teaching while I lurk about, trying to be unobvious," Liz says.

"I never thought that I would need a bodyguard."

"Don't think of me as a guard, think of me as a family member come to visit. Just try to help me do my work by following my instructions. I understand that you have an assistant at the school?"

"Yes Ann, she has helped me for years and if the pistol hadn't misfired might have interrupted my kidnapping."

"In the morning we will see to the pistols. Do you still have the stiletto and sheath?"

"Yes."

"I would like you to wear it until this is over. I have mine," she says flipping her skirt up to show the slim knife riding on her inside thigh."

Bertha again reddens at this woman's brazenness, then tells herself to relax as she goes to her room and retrieves the equipment. That the move is a practiced one, meant to distract any observer, while the woman pulls the weapon hasn't occurred to Bertha. When Liz has her place the knife and sheath and flips her skirts in the same fashion, Bertha catches on. "Why didn't you teach me that before?"

"We didn't know if you could be comfortable with the idea so we just hoped for the best."

"Does that mean you think I could need to use it?"

Liz just looks her in the eyes then turns away not wishing to discuss what she thinks is a dangerous situation, thinking that the men have been way to cavalier about things. Before David had left she had made her thoughts known and now she knows her job will be easier if Bertha is not made aware of the danger she could be in. The female agent knows that if the British send trained agents that they will kill to avoid being identified, and that they will not take a chance on amateurs bungling things, this time.

"Keep alert to anyone around you and don't let them take you no matter what, is the best I can tell you."

Bertha knows the implications are that if she is taken they would probably extract the information they seek and then dispose of her. She has a sudden appreciation for the amateurs sent the first time.

Chapter Twelve
Happiness at Last

The following week two men are seen arriving at Brink's inn. They take rooms for an undetermined length of time and ask a few questions about the area. A few hours after checking in they regain their mounts and ride down river. Shortly thereafter a man, who had been hanging around the bar, rides off in the same direction. By supper time all three have returned and eat in the dining room. Early next morning the two again leave on horse back with another 'tail' following soon after.

Later that day when the stage arrives from Cooperstown a rather elegantly dressed couple descends. Asking for Mr. Jewell's office, they are directed to the building next to the inn. Richard and the Houghtaling boy Robert, are working on survey maps as the couple walk in. Richard makes them comfortable in his office and soon learns that they have been to Richard Cooper's office and found it somewhat wanting in organization so they had come on to McDonald's Mills in their quest for the right property.

Introducing himself and his companion as Hugh and Joanna Moore, an acquaintance of Mr. Lansing, the lawyer that had employed James so many years ago, the newcomer quickly gets to his business in the area. Tugging his waistcoat down over his somewhat protruding stomach he states, "We are looking for land upon which can be built a sizeable lake to be developed as a resort location. I represent a group of investors. While Otsego Lake had met a lot of the criteria the quantity of land desired was not readily available. Besides, I have come expecting to have to build our own lake in order to accomplish the design we have in mind. I apologize for not contacting you prior to showing up. We had written Mr. Cooper and were assured that things would be in order. When they proved to be otherwise, Joanna and I decided to take Mr. Lansing's suggestion and stop by here also," Moore explains.

Bertha

Richard says, "The hills and streams near here offer many opportunities to build sizeable bodies of water, perhaps we can begin showing you some in the morning? Might I ask where you intend to spend the night?"

"We were recommended to Brink's inn."

"A fine choice, Aaron and his sons run a fine establishment. I will call for you about 8 AM and will have arranged for a mount for you."

"If you don't mind, arrange one for my wife also, she will accompany us."

"Certainly, consider it done. And if I may be so bold, I would like to invite you to my home for dinner tomorrow after our ride."

"We would be delighted, wouldn't we dear?" Mr. Moore directs at his wife.

"Most certainly so, and can you provide me with a regular saddle? I will be wearing breeches for our excursion into the forest. A dress can be so difficult. I look forward to meeting Mrs. Jewell."

"Then its all set. I'll see you at eight, it should be a fine day for a ride," Richard says, rising to shake Moore's hand and show them to the door, "While you get settled in, Robert and I will examine our maps for appropriate sites. Delighted to have met you Mrs. Moore, I hope you enjoy our little hamlet."

That night at dinner Richard tells Bertha and Elizabeth about the clients and the plans for tomorrow. Liz asks several questions about them. Then assured they fit the typical client profile, except for the quality of their dress, she offers to start the early preparations for dinner so Bertha need not leave school early.

It had been decided that Liz would not hang in the school but would be nearby should circumstances warrant. She had taken the time to give both Ann and Bertha some practice with the pistols, and then saw to it that the weapons were properly charged and placed in the school where they would be available to the women. All had agreed that the school door would be secured at all times and only opened to outsiders that are known. Thusly, Liz is able to wander about the neighborhood seemingly disinterested in the school while, in fact, watching for anyone who might approach the building.

Because Ann's home sets where it provides a view of the school, out the back and across the creek an easy rifle shot away, Liz has quietly arranged with Ann that loaded weapons are in a back bedroom with a view of the school. Her fellow agents in the area have been made aware of these arrangements should a siege of the schoolhouse be necessary.

It being well away from other buildings and with only one door the team has decided that should the enemy try to snatch Bertha, they prefer that it occur at the school as it can be sealed off quickly. The thick log walls would protect occupants from bullets yet no one could leave without those outside knowing. It is expected that to avoid being seen any abduction team would strike as before, after school has let out. Hopefully Bertha's protectors can detect any attempt and move into place to thwart it.

Morning finds Richard, Robert and the Moore's riding up the Oneonta Creek valley when Bertha opens the school. The two strangers have ridden out to the Charlotte valley early with one of their 'shadows' close behind. This time, David moves in as a second 'shadow', his team not sure that these two mean any harm, as each day they ride out to a different area walk about it a couple of hours, then return to the inn. So far any attempt to ascertain their reason for being here has been fruitless.

Liz has wandered about the area enjoying the beauty, accompanied by a pair of red-tailed hawks circling overhead. Their screeching calls becoming routine to anyone around. As the day has waned, Liz has worked her way up the hill nearly to the Jewell home where she can look down upon the schoolhouse and across the valley at "Oneonta'. From this vantage point she can see nearly any movement in the valley near the hamlet. Here and there farmers and others go about the daily routine. Nothing interrupts the serenity so she rises and heads to Bertha's kitchen to start the dinner meal. She is to build the fire next to the oven so a chicken which she is about to catch and behead can be roasted. up on the Oneonta Creek Richard and his clients are finishing their observations. Down at the school a lively discussion of 'women's rights' has just concluded, sure to stir the community when retold at the many supper tables.

"That was stimulating!" Ann remarks.

"I intend it to be," Bertha says, "We must make it a point that our students understand what 'establish justice' in the preamble of the Constitution should mean to the women of this country. Women are a part of this country, an important part that have participated in the fight for Independence as well as its defense on the frontiers. Our contributions must be recognized by making us equals."

"I was not surprised that most of the boys seem to reflect their fathers' views. If we change any of their thinking I will be surprised," Ann retorts.

"We may not change any of the older ones, but we are making them and the younger ones think about what is proper and that is going to be necessary before real change takes place," Bertha says, "This is only a start to a long process. We will probably reap some resistance but if we remain steadfast someday the women of this country will obtain their rightful place. I thank you for working with me on this."

"I am not going to attract a new husband by being for 'women's rights' but I feel that I could do more for Katherine and myself by taking on this task," Ann says.

"As long as I'm alive you will have an ally and as for a husband, I think one is in your future sooner that you think."

"Just as long as it isn't someone else's!" Ann smiles back.

"That David just might be a good prospect?" Bertha comments with a smile.

"You know, I believe I saw him ride by a few nights ago, I could not sleep and was looking out the front when a man came riding down your road."

"Probably just one of the team guarding us," Bertha says.

"Whether it was him or not, I wouldn't mind him riding by anytime," Ann observes with a grin.

"I'll see if it can't be arranged!"

"Why Bert, how you talk! Soon I hope before my reputation as a troublemaker reaches him."

"You think that is more important then your reputation as a husband killer .... Oh, forgive me! I speak without thinking!"

"No need to apologize! I know you mean me no harm and I must live with the fact. I only hope for a chance to explain before I'm judged."

"Well, you know that I don't judge you. I do believe its time I got on home to get dinner ready for Richard's guests."

Down in the hamlet Richard is just giving his client directions to the house on Panther Mountain. They go to their room to freshen up and change for dinner. Richard sees the horses to the stable and arranges for a buggy to be used that evening by his guests.

Bertha arrives in her kitchen to find that the chicken has been plucked and dressed for roasting. She proceeds to bake some fresh biscuits and chop up some fresh greens for vegetables. Liz has dressed for dinner while Bertha prepares the meal then she takes her turn at freshening up and dressing in one of the more elegant dresses she had used last at the Collingsworth dinner party. While she is doing this, Richard arrives home and gets ready to entertain his guests. He is sure that completing a deal with Moore could lead to other lucrative opportunities.

By the time that a buggy and team is heard in the front yard, the house is fragrant with the smell of roasted chicken and fresh baked biscuits.

Greeting his guests on the front porch, Richard escorts them into the house. They sweep into the front parlor and are greeted with as elegant a vision one could expect in the person of Bertha with Liz standing a few feet to her rear.

Hugh's bow upon being introduced is much lower and more protracted than ordinary. "Why how very lovely you are Mrs. Jewell," he speaks softly, giving her hand a squeeze as he does. "This is my wife, Joanna."

She sweeps forward, hand extended, "I'm delighted, what a lovely home you have. And that view from the porch, breathtaking! I do believe I saw that dress in my favorite shop in New York City."

"And well you might have," Richard interjects, "My wife often visits the city in order to keep us country bumpkins properly clothed."

Acknowledging their graciousness, Bertha turns to her companion and introduces her as a visiting cousin from South Carolina. Exchanging handshakes with each Liz takes an extra moment to look into each pair of eyes and sees nothing of concern there.

"Is that roast chicken I smell?" Hugh asks.

"Just fresh out of the oven, sir, and if you will take your place at the table we will serve it," Bertha answers.

"Brinks served an adequate meal last evening but nothing to compare to this if the smell is any indication. And a day of riding and hiking about has stimulated my appetite; let us enjoy ourselves before engaging in further conversation."

Down at Brink's the two riders have returned and as usual are at the same table partaking of an early supper. The 'shadows' have held back and once they are sure that they are set for the evening withdraw to near the river to meet with David.

Concern is that the two men are acting as a distraction to draw any guard on Bertha away. If that is so then what is the main thrust of the operation? Each man in turn retells what he has witnessed while tailing the duo. David listens intently and when melded in with what he has not seen in his travels around the area it becomes increasingly evident that either there is no operation in motion or that despite their best efforts they have missed any giveaway clues. At times like these David always likes to have Liz's input, finding her instincts to be invaluable when the evidence is contrary to that expected. But she is at the

Jewell home attending dinner for Richard's client. Then it hit him. What do they know about this client?

A comparison of notes makes David aware that it is possible that careful timing of appearances had distracted his team from any in depth evaluation of Richard's client. That any such avenue of approach might be tried to gain access to the Jewell household had been completely overlooked. David has a bad feeling in his gut.

He sends the two agents to Ann's to ask her to allow them to observe the road from her home, knowing that additional firearms were available there. They have instructions not to let anyone down the hill past them. He rides to Brink's to see what he can learn about the Moores.

A quick look in the dining room assures him that the two men are still there. He then slips down the hallway to the room the Moores are signed in to. A quick, practiced movement gets him past the lock. Once inside he rifles quickly through their things and finds nothing to raise suspicions. That alone raises his as practically nobody travels without some papers or items that point to their intent in the area. This collection was too 'clean' and it sets off an alarm that a less experienced person might miss. Slipping out he rechecks the dining room. The two men are gone.

Up the stairs to the room they share, he presses his ear to the door, all is quiet. They are not there, then where?

Trying not to draw attention to himself, David moves quickly to the stables where the man on duty says that two men just rode out toward the river crossing.

Running to his horse he intends to follow. Across the river David's two agents are surprised when two men ride up the hill in the darkness. Not prepared for traffic from the hamlet they have to let the dark figures proceed. A few minutes later David rides up.

With knowledge that the two mystery men have ridden toward the Jewell home in the dark, David is sure that an operation is underway. How to collapse it and obtain the captives Palmer has directed him to catch?

Bertha

To assure that his team is not detected he decides to leave the horses here at Ann's and proceed up hill through the forest. Spreading them out to his right he walks up the hill just in from the road so no one can descend it without detection.

Around the dinner table the food has been consumed with great gusto. The two men have retired to near the fireplace for a smoke. Bertha and Liz have made to carry the remains into the kitchen. Mrs. Moore has taken up a position a few steps from the kitchen door and when Bertha returns she finds herself staring at a pistol a few inches from her face.

"Say nothing," Mrs. Moore whispers and waits for Liz to appear.

Over by the fireplace her companion has another pistol pushed into Richard's ribs, "Keep quiet," he warns.

Striding into the dining area, Liz is surprised by the pointed pistol and sudden command, "Hands over your head." In a moment the situation has changed from genial dinner party to one of great danger.

Seeing that his companion has control of the two women, Richard's captor says, "Both of you come here and set straddle this bench, back to back." He waves his pistol to indicate where he wants them. Taking her pistol so he can guard all three he directs his companion to find something to tie their hosts up with. She returns with some lengths of rawhide and commences to tie the two women securely. That done he has Richard get on the floor and she ties his hands and feet so that all he can do is wiggle about. The sounds of hooves can be heard in the yard. "Our friends have arrived Hugh," the female offers, checking out the front window. She taps on the glass to let the new arrivals know that all is under control in the house.

"Not to be a ungracious guest, Mrs. Jewell, but we don't have a lot of time and I'm sure you know what we want. Give us the names of your handlers and answer our other questions or we start extracting the information by force. That was a delicious meal, by the way."

"I have no idea of what you refer, sir!"

"Don't play coy, we will not wait long for you to comply." Stepping in front of Liz he says, "Too bad you had to come visiting just now but perhaps you can help me convince your cousin to talk." With that he backhands Liz across the face with a blow that nearly knocks both women into the fireplace.

Grabbing their bindings, the female accomplice pulls them upright, "I suggest you talk, he gets ugly when he's in a hurry."

"Somebody around here killed two of my agents, I want what they came for then I intend to even the score. Make it easy and I'll be merciful, fight me and you all die in great pain."

"Tell him nothing," Liz snarls, spitting blood where he has split her lip.

"Oh what have we here? Perhaps you are more involved than I thought. Could you be part of the guard provided the schoolmarm?"

"Some schoolmarm, spying on good, loyal British subjects and their friends! Did you really think that you could weasel your way into their good graces then spill the goods to somebody in the American government? We mean to get even for all the persons put in prison or run out of the country. Who ran your operation? I want the name now!" He raises his hand as if to strike Bertha.

"Don't touch her you animal!" shouts Richard.

"And you keep quiet'" Hugh says, aiming a kick at Richard's mid-section. The air knocked out of him, her husband can only glare at his antagonist.

"I'm the one you want to get even with," Liz tries to draw his anger. Knowing they could die any minute, she attempts to draw Hugh's anger in an attempt to delay his executing either Richard or Bertha before help arrives.

"You, I know nothing about, but this little morsel has been described by several important people as the probable spy that gave up my uncle's organization on Long Island. I want the other names but intend to kill her and you with or without the information," he states holding a hand full of Bertha's hair and bending her head back in pain.

"You're wrong. Your organization missed my participation and I was the one that fingered them. Bertha was only used as a distraction so I could do my work," Liz testifies rather matter-of-factly.

Momentarily uncertain, he turns away thinking about the possibilities. Deciding that in the end it would make no difference, he turns back to the women intending to shoot Liz first. She, intently watching his eyes immediately knows his intent and throws all her weight and strength to force her and Bertha off the bench and into the female accomplice's legs. Her attempt works, knocking the woman to the floor and her pistol flying. Hugh's pistol discharges at thin air.

Moving as fast as reasonable but not wanting to give away their presence, David's team approaches the house undetected. At the front porch are two horses tied to the hitching rail and two men having a smoke set on the steps. Afraid that the horses might give their presence away he has one man stay in the yard hidden by some bushes while he and the other man circle and approach the house from the rear.

Slipping in through the unguarded kitchen, David and his companion have stood in the dark and heard Liz's statement. Knowing that she would make such remarks only as a last desperate resort the two men have stepped into the great room just as Liz has thrown herself and Bertha into the female abductor. Her pistol has slide to David's feet.

With the sound of Hugh's pistol the men on the front steps have stood up. One has dove for the front door only to be driven back with two bullets in his chest. The other, a little slower, has heard the command from behind him to halt and wishing to live another day, does as commanded.

Both Liz and Bertha are trying to hold onto their female antagonist and keep her from the pistol. It takes a few moments before every one in the room understands what has happened.

David has dropped his empty pistol and bent for the one at his feet, he now holds it pointed at Hugh. "Well, well, if it isn't Sir Hugh Moore of his majesty's Royal Army, and out of uniform at that! John is going to be very delighted at this catch. And the ever lovely Joanna Stark another great catch for us. Too bad your agent showed so much enthusiasm in your service. I'm afraid we did him great harm, referring to the corpse in the yard. It looks like we have caught a minor player as well, not bad for a night that started out badly."

Indicating that his associate should bring his prisoner in, David stands guard as the bindings are removed from Bertha and Liz as well as Richard and then applied to the three captives. "Do you have a secure room we can keep our guests in?" David asks Richard who stands rubbing where the rawhide has chafed his wrists.

"The woodshed out back is tight and stout."

"Then if you don't mind, please lead the way and our friends will follow," David waves the pistol in a way to indicate what he expects of the captives. Passing through the kitchen, Richard retrieves and lights a lantern as he leads the way to the woodshed. "Yes, yes. This will do just fine! I'm sure our guests will still be here come morning and to assure that, I and my associates will stand watches."

With that the three are pushed into the shed and the door closed and barred behind them. "Sorry for the crowded conditions but it is early winter and you would expect a woodshed to be full. I'm sure you all can work things out."

By the time the men have returned to the kitchen the women have gotten some tea brewing and they all gather around the table to relax. Just as they are setting down a breathless Ann comes rushing in, a pistol in each hand. She stands taking in the tranquil scene, gasping for breath, her face flush from the exertion, her bosom heaving.

"I heard the gun fire and came to make sure you are safe!" she addresses to Bertha, through ragged breaths.

"Oh yes, my wonderful friend, we all are well and in one piece thanks to the timely interference of David and his associates! But you, you seem about done in?"

"I went to the school for these pistols," which she holds dangling in each hand, "And ran all the way up not knowing what I would find!" her air coming better now.

David steps to her and takes the pistols. "Good to know we had such a beautiful and brave back up." He bows to the disheveled and sweating Ann, who blushes under his steady gaze.

Bertha embraces her friend and steers her to an empty chair. "Set and catch your breath my brave heroine."

"I will send one of my men to fetch John in the morning and the other to report to your sheriff. He should know that this will probably be the end of things. Once John and help arrive we will remove the prisoners and you good folks can get on with your lives."

Giving away her interest in him Ann asks David, "Must you leave with them?" Then realizing what she has done her face flushes a deeper red with further embarrassment.

Looking at the fire in her eyes and the flush on her face and bosom, David suddenly sees Ann as a woman and not just a player in the maelstrom of his life. Something tugs at his heart and a smile spreads across his usual stern countenance. "I guess John could do without me for a few days," he allows.

Bertha jumps up and says, "Good, you will be our guest for as long as you like!" Richard nods his approval. Ann feels a peace come over her she has not felt since Katherine's birth. Going to Richard, Bertha embraces him and says, "Maybe now we can live peacefully and raise our children with only the normal fears associated with life. And yes, my husband, we are going to have a baby," she says to his astonishment and glee.

Jumping to his feet, Richard encases her in a great hug, "How such a bad day can turn into such a happy night I cannot say, but to have good friends about as I receive this news makes me happy beyond all words!"

Bertha too, feels a flush of peace come over her, "That I can give you children will be my greatest joy. That we can share our good fortune with close friends in this great country will be a future worth the price of the past."

ACKNOWLEDGEMENTS

Earlier books in this series kept very close to the historical timeline, this portion of the narrative reflects the historical happenings of the times but plays loose with the timeline in order to weave the story. One glaring example is the great flood the occurred in 1816 the same year when Summer 'never happened'.

Other historical events are listed in the TIMELINE but not referred to in the narrative. This is done to help the reader maintain a perspective of important events that occurred during the story's timeline. Often events occurring great distances away have a way of driving local happenings.

APPENDIX

HISTORICAL TIMELINE

1803 – President Jefferson purchases the Louisiana Territory from France doubling the size of the country.

1804 – 1806 – Lewis & Clark explore the newly purchased territory bringing back tales of mountains and valleys full of vast natural resources.

1805 – McDonald brothers bought the mills from the VanDerwerkers and moved them on to the Silver Creek.

1806 – Hamlet called McDonald's Mills, Full Eclipse of the sun, June 16th.

1807 – USS Chesapeake fired upon by HMS Leopold as the British continue to 'press' American sailors, June.

1808 – James Madison elected President of the United States, Dec.

1811 – Battle of Tippecanoe, Nov.

1812 – War breaks out with Great Britain. NY State legislature passed country's first public education law.

1816 – Year of the great flood that changed the course of the Susquehanna in many places and the 'Summer that never was'.

1817 – McDonald opens a post office in his tavern, hamlet named Milfordville, officially.

1830 – Town of Oneonta formed from parts of the towns of Otego and Milford.

1832 – Village of Milfordville changed to Village of Oneonta.

BIBLIOGRAPHY

Cooper, James Fenimore, Wyandotte', State University of New York Press, 1982

Campbell, Dudley M., A History of Oneonta, G.W. Fairchild & Co., 1906

Gibson, Herbert A., Arrowheads, Fences, and Iron Horses, A History of the Town of Oneonta, Unicorn Publication Printers, 1976

Beers, F.W., Atlas of Otsego Co., NY, NY; F.W. Beers, A.D. Ellis & G.G. Soule, 1868

Alan Taylor, William Cooper's Town, Vintage Books, 1996

Louis C. Jones, Growing up in the Cooper Country, Syracuse University Press, 1965

By extension

Levi Beardsley, Reminiscences,

&

Henry Clarke Wright, Human Life

James Arthur Frost, Life on the Upper Susquehanna, 1783-1860, King's Crown Press, 1951

INTERNET SEARCH ENGINE

Google®

INTERNET WEB SITES

http://www.
rootsweb.com/~nyotsego/oneontahistory1.html
/oneontahistory2.html
/history.htm
/~usgenweb/ny/Otsego/census/1800/0026b.gif
/0027b.gif
/0028a.gif
/0030b.gif
external.oneonta.edu/cooper/articles/nyhistory/
1968nyhistory-pickering.html
/1954nyhistory-butterfield.html
/1979nyhistory-pickering.html
/1991nyhistory-taylor.html
oneonta.k12.ny.us/rs/localhistory.htm
thedailystar.com/opinion/columns/simonson/2003/11/
simonson1122.html
oneonta.ny.us/history.htm
fortklock.com/revolutionstoriesmckean.htm
/timeline1779.htm
usgennet.org/usa/ny/county/Otsego/book/morris/
pioneers.html
/laurens/settlers.html
/coop/coop1stpt2.htm
/coop/coop1stpt1.htm
/coop/coop/coopmisc.htm
/tryon/
nysm.nysed.gov/albany/bios/l/adlansing3695.html
encyclopedia.com/html/section/
Livngstn_HenryBrockholstLivingston(1757-1823)
hopefarm.com/otsegony.htm
rabies.mnr.gov.on.ca/history.cfm

viable-herbal.com/singles/herbs/s405.htm
vet.purdue.edu/depts/addl/toxic/plant28.htm
cdc.gov/ncidod/dvrd/rabies/natural_history/nathist.htm
iaw.on.ca/~awoolley/brang/brang.html
ushistory.org/march/timeline.htm
bvma.org/tryon4/history.html
wordiq.com/definition/ History of New York
history.rochester.edu/canal/bib/Campbell/Chap02.html
thetwinters.com/generalsullivan/newton.htm
collections.ic.gc.ca/heirloom series/volume3/chapter4/69-74.htm
tolatsga.org/iro.html
germantown.k12.il.us/html/woodland2.html
motherbedford.com/Indian5.htm
teachervision.fen.com/lesson-plans/lesson-2120.html
u-s-history.com/pages/h1214.html
canoeregatta.org/faq.htm
newton.dep.anl.gov/natbltn/200-299/nb257.htm
theweatheroutlook.com/commview/article.asp?id=188
wilkes.edu/~kirbypl/river.html
house.gov/Constitution/Constitution.html
ulysses.ny.us/trumansburg.html
fortpittmuseum.com/History.html
home.earthlink.net/~gfeldmeth/chart.1812.html
memory.loc.gov/ammem/odmdhtml/pptime.html
aboutflags.com/shop/

MAPS

http://www.
fortklock.com/Iroquois1776.JPG
            /JohnsonRaid.htm
            /province.JPG
            /Harrison.htm
            /patentheadwaterss.htm
            /patentsSouth.htm
            /patentmap1.htm
docs.unh.edu/NY/onoe18ne.jpg

/NY/coop09ne.jpg
/NY/hrtw12se.jpg
terraservervice.net/image

Map of The Town of Oneonta, Atlas of Otsego Co., 1868

The page #76 map from the A & S Railroad Map Book

Orthophoto Maps # 204/205 & # 205/206 of a portion of the Susquehanna Valley, 1973

SPECIAL ACKOWLEDGEMENTS

Ada Drake, Claire Kemper and Ruth Kukenberger of the Otsego County, State of New York, Clerk's Office for invaluable help with historic maps of Otsego County.

Dolores 'Dollie' Baldwin, my wife, for her loving patient encouragement.

ISBN 141207036-8